Love Letters to Writers

ENCOURAGEMENT, ACCOUNTABILITY, AND TRUTH-TELLING

Andi Cumbo-Floyd

Edited by Laurie Jensen
Cover Design by Stephanie Spino
Book Layout ©2017 BookDesignTemplates.com

.

Love Letters to Writers/ Andi Cumbo-Floyd. —1st ed.

ISBN 978-0-692-96080-6

Contents

Table of Contents

Dedicated to the Members of our Online Writing Community, who always encourage, always challenge, and always strive for the truth

How we spend our days is, of course, how we spend our lives.

—Annie Dillard

I ♥ Writers

Dear Beautiful People,

Over two years ago, I started writing weekly letters to the folks in the online writing community I coordinate. (You're MOST welcome to join us.) Because I knew these people—some of them quite well—the letters were personal; both as I thought of them and the moments of their writing lives, and for me, since I knew I could trust them with some of the rawest, most real parts of my life as a writer.

At the suggestion of one of those community members, the talented and kind Amanda Cleary Eastep, I have chosen what I feel are the most powerful, most honest, most vulnerable, most true letters I can from the over 100 I wrote to the community members—while slipping a couple from my larger newsletter and blog in there, too.

My hope is that you will find encouragement, perhaps a little nudge to do your work, and some companionship in your writing journey as you read the letters. There are fifty-two, so you could—

if you have far more stamina and patience than I—read one a week. Or you could binge them all in an evening.

Whatever way you read these words, I hope you will take hope, comfort, and a little energy to keep at this writing thing from them.

Much love,
Andi

CHAPTER 2

Go Wild!

Dear Beautiful People,

Just now, over the top of our barn and through the pines beyond, the sun is rising in the brightest of yellows against the steel-white winter sky. He's not shy, this guy. He's burning with all the brightness he can muster, and we are grateful—for the way his presence is used to bring us life.

I wonder if maybe the best thing we can do as writers is to burn the same way when we draft our work . . . to let it all go, to write without boundaries, without worrying about who we might burn, about what we look like, about how the light of our words hits someone. We just write wild . . . big and wild, like a fire.

I've said it before, and I'll probably say it one thousand times— the brain is not the place from which we get our best word-energy. That energy lives in the heart, and often, to get at the heart, we have to let our brains take a break, step to the rear, steep in silence a bit. When we are trying to control, manipulate, anticipate, we are thinking—we are girding—we are worrying . . . and worry has no place in the fire of first drafts.

There will be time enough for worry, to gain control, to tame the fire later.

But now, in the first stages of writing, we need to write WILD, our arms flung wide as we spin with the words. Wild and free.

So that's my challenge for you—live into that much-rephrased axiom of writing: write hot; edit cold. In that draft, let your characters, your language, your passion, your emotion burn white hot . . . Later you can come apply the cool, controlled light of reason. But now, let it all go . . . be wild. Big and wild.

What keeps you from writing wild in your drafts? What holds you back? What do the ugly voices whisper? What might it feel like to let go?

Much love,
Andi

CHAPTER 3

Writing the In-Between

Dear Beautiful People,

Today is Martin Luther King, Jr. Day in the US. It's one of my favorite holidays because it honors a man who fought to do great good and who, still, made big mistakes. I appreciate a person who is real, especially in our glossy times.

I've been thinking about this gloss, this "black and white" thinking, if you'll forgive the pun on this day, this need to have precision and answers and "do this" instead of "try this."

We live in unforgiving times, and that rigid "get it right the first time" mindset can silence writers quicker than almost anything. I expect you all know that.

So here's my challenge to you: write in the betweens, the spaces between right and wrong, do this and not that. The liminal openings that exist in gray sometimes and in rainbow colors of magnificence at others.

As you look back at your life for your memoir, give yourself grace for your mistakes and lay them out for the reader. Don't disguise them as half-truths or veil them under the bravado of false righteousness.

As you lean into your characters, give them openings where they can show they are whole in their brokenness. Let them make bad choices and then regret them, and let them love imperfectly.

As you craft poems from twigs and tinfoil, let the disruption of rhythm and rhyme bounce you and your readers to higher understanding. Choose just the wrong word from time to time.

As you build books to help other people, admit the gaps in your knowing, show your work, forgive your mistakes so that the people you advise will forgive their own.

Not a one of us does this living perfectly—Dr. King plagiarized his dissertation and had a pretty wretched series of relationships with women other than his wife, and yet, that does not diminish the power of his words when he says, "Let us develop a kind of dangerous unselfishness."

Dangerously unselfish, my friends. I think that's what we need to be as writers. People not interested in girding up our rightness or projecting some false sense of correctness. People interested, instead, in digging into the meaty betweens where beauty and pain rub shoulders, and where truth and forgiveness are bedfellows.

Where might you need to let yourself fall more into the betweens? Where might you need to peel back either/or and settle for, well, just this?

Much love,
Andi

CHAPTER 4

Publishing Books Makes Me Uncomfortable, but That's Okay

Dear Beautiful People,

I have this chair—a recliner—where I sit to sew. I call it my "nest." My mom had one, and now I've followed in her footsteps. A good lamp. My sewing basket and lots of yarn at hand. A blanket. And right now, the spring's seed catalogs are stacked next to it, too. It's my comfortable spot, my refuge.

Sometimes, I'd rather not leave it. I can read there, sew there, watch TV there, even sleep there if need be. It's molded to me now . . . it holds me up in the easiest way.

Lately, my chair has been beckoning more and more because I'm doing something that is uncomfortable and really quite hard for me: I'm publishing a book.

I'm a writer. I enjoy time alone. I like to ruminate and stew and ponder. I enjoy hours of solitude when I can work and think and stare out the window. In many, many ways, I like to be hidden.

I imagine some of you are like that, too. You prefer the internet to the telephone, the office with walls over the cubicle. The wandering solo walk to the group run.

I've never read the statistics on that, but I imagine many of us writers are introverts. I certainly am.

So publishing feels uneasy to me, challenging, disingenuous in some ways. Still, I do it . . . and I do it for one simple reason—I **believe in what I write.**

I can't tell you what exactly gives me that confidence since I'm terrified that my writing is banal nonsense, and I'm not really willing to pin down what my books mean for anyone else but myself. But I do believe in them, with all my heart. I trust that they are important, even if I can't say why.

Therefore, I publish, even when it makes me squirm, and along the way, I have found that squirming is a good thing.

Here are five ways that publishing teaches me things I can't learn from my recliner.

- Spending money helps. In the past, I've tried to do much of this independent publishing gig on my own, but this time, I'm hiring some folks.
- I have to ask for help. If you've read anything at all about launching a book, you know that having a team of folks behind you is important, and boy, am I relying on this team! I ask them to share things, give me advice, and generally rally around this baby of mine. I am not awesome at that . . .I prefer to think I can go it alone. (See #1.)
- I have to learn new things and actually do them. I LOVE reading books about new experiences and skills, and I typically resent having to implement things,

particularly hands-on things. But nothing makes me try something new like believing in my book . . . (See #4.)

- I make mistakes. Doing something new means I may make mistakes. I might flub something up royally or put off some folks or lose subscribers. But every mistake is a lesson so that I can do this publication thing better next time.

- I have to cede control. No matter how many people I hire to work with me, no matter how wonderful my launch team, no matter how many new strategies for promotion I try, no matter how many mistakes I take to heart, ultimately, I have no control over whether anyone at all reads my book. That's a hard thing, a sleepless night kind of thing, but it's an important lesson—for publication, and for life.

So far, so good on this publication, but man, oh man, do I want to hunker down in that recliner with some yarn, a quilt, and eighteen episodes of *Supernatural*. I won't, though . . . because I believe in *Steele Secrets*, and I want you to know about her, imperfect beauty that she is.

Much love,
Andi

CHAPTER 5

The Gift of Literary Citizenship

Dear Beautiful People,

Right now, I'm feeling all the love of our larger literary community . . . friends have edited my book (for pay, of course) and will format it, too. Another friend designed my book cover and another did the book trailer. And many, many more (including many of you) have bought copies, contacted me about interviews for blogs, shared the order link, and just told me kind things about Mary and her story. I feel girded up in this work.

And because I know this feeling, I do my best to help provide it for other people by celebrating their publications, ordering their books as much as budget allows, sharing their news and stories on social media, and just generally celebrating their accomplishments.

But my friend Karrie, http://www.karriehiggins.com/,she is the SUPERSTAR of literary citizenship. When my earlier book came out, she walked—she has epilepsy so she can't drive— all around Salt Lake City asking libraries and bookstores to order the book. She shares news of my publications, and she champions every bit of writing I do . . . and she does that for dozens of writers. She is my hero.

I imagine you all have felt this in some way—the jolt of confidence that comes when a friend congratulates you or reads the book when they said they would. And I imagine that you—like me— have also felt the sag of disappointment when that doesn't happen.

So this week, my encouragement to you is that you step beyond your own writing goals (and that can be really hard to do, believe me). and look for a way you can support another writer. Maybe share something they've written. Maybe buy a book. Maybe just send them a tiny note to say, "Keep going." They will appreciate it . . . and your soul will feel good.

Plus, a bonus— when you do this for other people, you'll find they are quick to do it for you, too.

Much love,
Andi

CHAPTER 6

Write What You Want to Know

Dear Beautiful People,

I'm going to be really honest here—I just ate a LOT of rice pudding for breakfast . . . and I don't even feel bad about it. My stress level is pretty high at the moment, and this gift of goodness—homemade with raisins—is a tiny lift to my weary soul.

Here's another thing that's lifting me up these days: the chance to start a new book. I've been feeling his life wedge itself into the spaces between my ribs for a while now, pretty much ever since I saw his name on a will, since I saw that he was—as were millions of others—given away like the antique sideboard.

His name is Montello. And in 1870, he lived near the farm where I now write. He still lived near this place, where he was enslaved.

He and the woman who was also enslaved here and who I call Judith are the focus of my next book . . . or at least my next researched book. I think I have a cozy mystery about a woman farmer in me first.

I want to know about the people who were enslaved on this place I now call home. I want to know their names if I can. I want to sketch their family trees. I want—Lord willing—to see their cheekbones in the faces of their descendants.

So, there—that's what I want to know, and the energy behind the curve of the question, it draws me forward even on this day when I am so very tired.

I suspect you all have things you want to know, too. Why do those words from one child on a playground forty years ago still hurt? Why are people so divided over Beyoncé's Super Bowl performance? Why do you hear a young boy who has never existed whispering stories about his toy dinosaur in your ear? Why do the male birds have brighter colors? Why do you take special joy in a rainy day?

My teacher, Sharman Apt Russell, calls those "fruitful questions." The questions that drive us, call us forward, poke at us over and over again, those are the ones she suggests we write into because there's life there. We don't have the answers all determined; we don't even know where the journey to the answer will take us. But the question compels us.

And if it compels us, it carries energy, and that energy will reach out from the pages and whisper to our readers, too.

So if you have questions, if you are uneasy, if you feel intense emotion about something which you do not yet understand, write there. See what you find. And share that journey of the question . . . you and your readers will find life there.

Much love,
Andi

CHAPTER 7

Write into the Unknown

Dear Beautiful People,

We are in the midst of a perfect snow this morning. It's light and gentle, and the hush of its tenderness is filling the farm this morning. The walnut tree outside the dining room is unshadowed by the gift of frozen flakes, and the birds—a red-headed woodpecker, some chubby juncos, and two sparrows—are flitting about in my view. Perfect.

This week, I've had conversations with several people about the uncertainty of writing, about the uneasiness many of us feel when we don't know where a project is going, about the unpredictability of book sales, about the risk we take when we tell certain stories. Every single one of those things can stop us cold . . . think Hans Solo frozen in *The Empire Strikes Back.* Except unlike Harrison Ford's character, we don't come out of that frozen state the same as we were.

Every time we step out of writing because of fear, because we can't predict what might happen, we make it not only harder to write that story but also harder to write anything. **When we give fear a bit of ground, it encroaches until it takes over our words and silences us completely.**

So this week, my gentle nudge for you is to embrace the unpredictability.

- Begin to write that novel even when you don't know where it's going. (There's BY FAR more energy in the unknowing than in the most carefully-plotted outline.)
- Get that hard story of your adolescence down, even if people might not like that you are recording the way they have wounded you. (You don't have to share it if you're not ready, after all.)
- Try that new poetry form that's haunting you even though you feel like formal poetry isn't your bag and you think rhyme is hokey.
- Delve deep into that advice you have to give and be willing to admit when you have failed.

The worst that's going to happen is that the story, memoir, poem doesn't work. But even that—as hard as it will be—isn't as bad as walking around with fear gagging your words. Trust me on that.

I'm holding out all the hope of wild, brave writing for you.

Much love,
Andi

CHAPTER 8

Leaning into What
We Cannot Control

Dear Beautiful People,

This morning, I began a new book. Or I should say, I re-began a book that I have begun twice before and may need to re-begin again. It may just be one of those start-and-stop projects.

But I read the words of Christie Purifoy this morning, and I listened deep to the whisper behind them . . . whispers that said, "Andi, you don't need to worry about the sales or about how the life of the farm will come to be . . . you only need to do the next thing, the thing you can do. You need to create and answer. You need to put aside the striving."

For the past month, I have been in the throes of a book launch. My focus has been on getting *Steele Secrets* into hands, and that's a necessary and good thing. Book marketing is a neutral thing. There's nothing wrong with telling people about our work and encouraging them to purchase it.

But I slid well past neutral and into desperate. I was consuming—for hours a day—advice on marketing my books. I was dreaming of days when I could watch the sales pay my bills. And I became greedy and unaligned to my purpose. I could feel it, but I wasn't really able to stop it . . . not at the moment. My momentum was too great.

Yet two friends told me something about an email I sent, two men who know me well. "That didn't sound like you, Andi." And I was buffeted back to myself by their kind accountability. Nudged home to what I know and trust.

I know really only one thing about writing books or anything else we send out into the world:

The only thing we control about writing is how we carve the words into the page.

We don't control how people read our words. We don't control how many copies we sell. We don't control whether or not an agent will want to represent us or an editor publish our work. We don't control the things people say about our work. **We only control the work itself.**

So I'm going back to work on a new book. A book about the farm, a book I may put down for other books, but a book I am tied to in ways I don't have words yet to explain.

More, though, I'm returning to what I do—write. I'm leaning in hard, letting the wind of words hold me upright because I know I can trust this work. I know I can trust it because I know I can trust the One who wrote the work into the very way I was made.

I don't know where you sit with your writing at this moment. I don't know if you're trying to puzzle together a plan or trying to get it right before you even begin to write. I don't know if you're about to launch a book or have one in the world that isn't selling as well as you'd like. I don't know if you are just starting out with submissions to literary journals and magazines or a few hundred pages laid out in journals. I don't know the way the walk of words will look for you, but I do know this with every woven fiber of my being: **If you lean in hard to the work before you, if you turn it with care and attention, if you pull honesty from the far corners of all of who you are, the rest is not yours to carry.**

Much love,
Andi

CHAPTER 9

You Can't Rush a Writing Life

Hi Beautiful People,

On Saturday, I lead a writers' retreat at the beautiful home of Kelly Chripczuk. Kelly and her husband John created a gentle, easy space for the gathering, and immediately, I saw people settle into comfort and rest because of that creation.

We talked writing and fear, stories, and control. We read our words. We cried a few tears. It was all lovely, easy, calm.

Then, at lunch, we began talking about blogging, about how to do it—platforms and hosting and such—and lots of us had lots of knowledge about lots of things. Without my really knowing how it happened, all the ease of the morning slipped into frenzy as we slid into talking about platforms and marketing and ALL THE WORK. I could see panic behind some folks' eyes, and I tried to temper it, tried to slow us down to say, as Kelly did, but you can start small and learn as you go. You don't have to do it all now.

Still, we were worked up. I could feel it . . .TOO MUCH TO DO . . . just the conversation about production had sent us very near an edge where we wouldn't be able to get back to the joy of creation that Kelly and I chose very carefully as the focus of this day.

After lunch, we did make it back to joy as we shared our work and did a workshop that felt like healing and testimony and a good, long walk all in one. At the end of the day, I felt light and hopeful, if exhausted.

But as I drove home that evening, a slew of book-publishing podcasts on my phone waiting, I pondered just what it is about NOW that makes us want to fill every minute with the things that can come then. Why the urgency to do it all now, do it all before we even know what our own voices sound like, when we even know what we have to say?

I suspect we end up focusing on all those things because they are easier. There is a method for setting up a website after all, and I can count how many times I share things on Facebook. It's much harder to figure out how I'm going to carve 1,000 words from oxygen and brain energy, and then it's even harder to figure out how I came to think that character's brother needs to barge in and what will come next. Doing is definitely easier than creating. (Note--doing is often very creative, too. I don't want to make a fine point of this distinction.)

Here's what I know about myself, though:

- Very few things make me as calm and centered as writing with focus, even if the writing isn't awesome and even if I have no idea what I will DO with it.
- I can tweet, post, share, like, and comment until I turn purple, and it may bring me nothing near as good as I can get when I write honest and true.
- I am not called to be a producer. I'm called to be a creator.

Now, that's not to say that we don't have to market or know about things like websites. We do. But those are the practical elements of a never-practical gift. And they have to come after, after we create . . . sometimes years after. Because we owe our creative work the best energy we have to give it.

Our people need our energies. Our homes need our energies. Our day jobs need our energies. But when we come to the time when we are looking at our creations, we need to give the creating FAR MORE than we do the selling.

So breathe, my friends. Many great resources exist for how to blog or market or sell, and those resources will be there when you need them. But you don't need them all now.

The only thing every day needs is your creativity, fresh and true as you can make it. The rest will come in time.

Much love,
Andi

CHAPTER 10

Who We Listen To

Dear Beautiful People,

Just now, I'm talking myself back into something I forget all the time: I know what's best for me and my writing life.

Just now, I'm reminding myself of what I need to be creative, of when I write best, of what my goals and dreams for this singular life of mine are.

Just now, I'm running hard up against all the things that other people—good, well-intentioned people—put out as the "should" of the writing life.

Just now, I'm trying to go inward and upward as I find my words waiting, where they always wait, just for me.

I don't know about you all, but I'm weary of writing advice. I'm weary of being told a writer should do this or not do this, should write here and not there, should write when and not then. I'm weary, too, of the way I glom onto those "shoulds" because I think that somehow, if I don them like weapons, if I bear them before me as shields, all of this writing stuff will be easy. As if just getting up at the right time, or owning the right journal, or preparing just this much space for this such thing will make the work of writing magical in every moment.

I know it won't.

But I know what does it for me . . . showing up at the page, reading some lines of poetry, picking up a pen that writes quick and smooth, and simply getting some words down. For me, that's the way forward.

For you, the way may be much different. It may involve hours of silence before you begin. It may include a block of time in a cabin at the edge of a glade. It may be the minutes during a nap when you capture the character or the language that has been spinning with you all day. It may be a 1:00 a.m. cup of tea at a second-story room overlooking the city.

For writing, there is no ONE WAY. There is only YOUR WAY, the way that gets your words onto paper and fills you at the same time.

Sometimes, it takes us years to find that way, and that's okay. We read advice and try it out. We toss some aside and pull some close. We craft our own doorway in. And sometimes we have to lock one door and build a new one.

I know this for sure—each of us has a different doorway into our own rooms in the big, wild house that is made of words. We test others' doors and find we can only get partway through or that they are locked to us entirely. So we take a bunch of colored pencils or some paints or that perfect-tipped pen, and we make our own door, the one that is just tall enough and just wide enough for us to walk through intact and whole.

And once we're in, we find our rooms of words, waiting and ready as silent or noisy, colorful or sedate, brightly-lit or candle-golden as we need.

Much love,
Andi

CHAPTER 11

What Are We Afraid Of?

Dear Beautiful People,

I have a cat who is terrified if any people are near. I've had her and her sister living with me for almost eight years now, and she's still terrified of me. Nothing I can do will coax her out. To be sure she's okay, I actually have to startle her out from her hiding place.

Sometimes, I think writers are a lot like Charlotte. We tuck ourselves into corners— be they journals or password-protected blogs or ideas about writing or writing books. We are so afraid that we only come out when startled, even though we really want to walk about in the world with our words unfurled.

I long ago learned that there is nothing I can do to coax other people out from their hiding from writing in general or from public writing in specific. Sometimes, it's hard enough to get myself to do it. Nothing I say will draw some of us out, and I'm not interested in frightening anyone into revealing themselves.

So, if you will, imagine me here, whispering to you in the same voice I still try to use with Charlotte. "It's okay. It's just me. You're safe." I'm just here to remind you that you are loved, no matter what—whether you step out boldly or choose to hide. You are never less loved.

Still, I hope you step out boldly with your words. I hope you push past your fear and take a few timid steps into the big room of the world that is waiting.

Perhaps a few reminders will help:

- Some people may be waiting to hear just what you have to say. Some people might NEED it. Books have, as I've said often, quite literally saved my life several times. Maybe yours will save someone else.
- The people who count in your evaluation of your own value are waiting to cheer you on, to support you, to say, YES!! (The people who don't do that need not have a place in your echelons of loved ones.)
- Sometimes what we say by way of "reasons" for why we aren't writing is just fear's crafty creation of excuses. A real reason for not writing is magnificent and temporary—a sudden illness, an injury, a massive project that comes up out of nowhere; an excuse for not writing is usually chronic and anticipatable. So your child's fever and subsequent need for your care— REASON. Your four hours of TV a night that leave you too tired to wake early to write, even though that's what you WANT to do—EXCUSE.

If we can turn our "reasons" for not writing and begin then with the phrase, "I'm afraid to write because . . . ," then we can be pretty sure we're dealing with excuses brought on by fear. What we say:

I'm too busy to write my book. What we mean: I'm afraid to write my book so I keep saying YES to other things.

My "reason" that's really an excuse: "I need to make more money, so I have to focus on 'building my business.'" Total excuse for me. Total way of giving into the fear of how hard writing is, of how much apathy my books will find when they come out.

I don't know what your excuses are—fear of people feeling neglected by you, fear of not having enough time to finish what you start, fear of not 'doing it right,' fear of having regrets that you gave time to something that was just for you first—but if your "reasons" for not writing are rooted in fear, trust me when I say, they are excuses, not real reasons. That doesn't mean they're not real or not burly in their power. It just means you can get past them, if you choose to do so.

Charlotte, my precious cat, can't tell me her fears. She can't explain what keeps her from exploring the great big world that is now open to her with her new cat door. But you can, and I hope you will. Sometimes, the easiest way to diminish a fear is to call it out for what it is and watch it shrink.

Much love,
Andi

CHAPTER 12

The Teeter-Totter of Discipline and Grace

Dear Beautiful People,

For the first time in several months, I achieved my goal of writing 1,000 words a day on my work in progress this week. Most mornings, I didn't want to do it. I had other things to do—things that pay me money and aren't as hard—but I did it. Each time, it took me less than thirty minutes. I draft very quickly because I've practiced for years, but my revision process is quite slow. When I was done, I felt great because I wasn't going to be carrying the burden of disappointment and guilt I feel when I don't write.

For me, writing is a calling, a vocation, my life's work, if you can bear that level of grandioseness and not think it some sort of April Fool's Day joke. (I assure you, I'm serious.) So when I'm not using it, I feel a bit like that servant from the parable who buries the money in the dirt. I don't like that feeling.

Over many years of practice, after reading many books on writing, through listening to many friends who are further down the path of words than I am, I have learned that a real key to writing is discipline, a regimented putting-of-the-butt-in-the-chair. I don't believe in inspiration. I believe in hard work, in showing up, in facing the page as often as possible to get the writing done.

But I also believe in grace. I believe that it's far more detrimental to my mental health if I walk around on the days I don't write feeling shameful about what I haven't done. I know that shame is too heavy a weight to bear when I need lightness to create. I am certain that no good (and almost no writing) comes from feeling weighed down by what didn't happen.

So here's how I keep the teeter-totter of discipline and grace for myself. (By the way, I am coming to think of balance as shifty, not something you pin down forever like a beautiful butterfly, but something we dance through during the various days and periods of our life. Hence, the teeter-totter metaphor.)

- **I have a regular goal for writing.** For me, that's 1,000 words a day five days a week. That goal is achievable for me on a daily basis.
- **I have a regular writing time for each of those five days.** Right now, that time is 6:00 a.m.because I can wake at 5:00, do a little reading, write, check email, and then feed the farm animals. That time will shift as the sunrise moves earlier this summer.
- **I give myself time off.** I don't write on weekends. That's my farm time, my time with Philip, my time to binge-watch *Firefly*. My time with family and friends. If I'm making space for things I love sometimes, I don't tend to skimp on writing, which I don't always love, the other times.
- **I look ahead to how I will make this time given what's happening in the rest of my life.** If I know I'm

traveling as I am this week) I evaluate whether or not I'll still be able to write that 1,000 words. If I don't see it as possible, I scratch that day off my calendar. But just that day. By looking ahead at what might make my goals hard to achieve, I give myself the space to not hit the goal that day without derailing myself with guilt for many days.

- **When I miss a writing day unexpectedly, I look at why that happened as soon and as honestly as possible.** Sometimes, I just don't get it done, and so when that happens, I take stock right away. Did an emergency arise? Was I sick? Or did I make choices that got in the way? If this was about choice, why did I make that choice? Am I okay with that choice? And if not, what will I do to make better choices to allow for my writing next time? I find that 90 percent of my missed writing days were my choice, and most of those choices I would like to not make again. So I adjust my schedule or my practices—like this week, I committed to not looking online until my 1,000 words were done. It worked well for me.

For you right now, five days a week may not be possible; 1,000 words may be too little or too much. Mornings may not work. You have to find what works for you.

I believe you have to make a goal and set a schedule that works for you, and then do all you can to keep to it. And I believe this is possible for everyone most of the time. You may be tempted to say that because you work a lot of hours you can't set a goal or schedule, or because you have young children you can't keep a schedule, or because you have a chronic illness you can't make a goal or keep a schedule, or because your second toe is longer than your big toe schedules don't work for you. I get it. Life is hard for all of us a lot of the time and in a lot of ways.

Here's the thing, though—people have written books while raising young children. People have written books while working to make partner at a law firm and working eighteen -hour days. People have written books while battling cancer for their lives. The way they do that may not be as fast as I do in my child-free, write-for-a-living daily life (which has its own griefs and challenges, I assure you), but they do it. And they do it by committing, by practicing, by prioritizing, and by giving themselves the grace to say, "Today was not the day, but I'll try again tomorrow."

So here's my **NO FOOLIN'** challenge for you.

- **Make a weekly writing goal.**
- **Set a weekly schedule for achieving that goal.**
- **Celebrate when you meet your schedule.**
- **Evaluate when you don't and let the "didn't" go.**
- **Try again the next day.**

What do you say? Are you in?

Much love,
Andi

CHAPTER 13

A Little Bit at a Time

Dear Beautiful People,

During the winter months, I watched something like forty-eight episodes of *Supernatural*. I have no guilt about that. This weekend, I started a new cozy mystery series about a cheese shop (Avery Aames is the author if you too think a small town, a gourmet cheese shop, and murder make a great combo.) I will read the whole series within weeks, no doubt. I'm a classic binger . . . as are many of us, I think.

Here's something I've learned, though—binging is okay for consumption, but not production . . . and definitely not for art . . . and most definitely not for my creative spirit. I cannot sit down and write for five hours straight. I cannot write a whole book in a day or even a weekend. (I realize some people do this, and maybe they're awesome, but I'm skeptical, I admit.)

For me, creating has to be more about rhythm and readiness, about flow and freedom, about practice and perseverance. It's a daily thing, and that daily practice shapes my life into a way of being that is about writing. When I write a little a day, I start noticing more, seeing with the eyes of a writer, listening for stories, paying attention to details.

Plus, in my life, it's easier to carve out fifteen to thirty minutes most days than it is to set aside two hours once in a while.

So here's my suggestion for you this week. It's really simple: **Slow and steady wins the race. And you're only racing yourself. The day's finish line is simply to be a better writer than you were yesterday. That's it.**

If you're someone like me who likes quantifiables, try these on:

- If you write 500 words (that's about two double-spaced pages) a day, you'll have a draft of a full-length book in three and a half months.
- If you write 1,000 words (that's about four double-spaced pages) a day, you'll have a draft of a full-length book in less than two months.

So slow and steady doesn't mean it'll take you forever. But it may mean that the weight of carrying the "not enough time to write" burden gets a little bit easier to bear.

Much love,
Andi

CHAPTER 14

The Embodied Writer

Dear Beautiful People,

Since January I have been wearing this purple Fitbit on my arm, a generous gift from my in-laws. I asked for the tool because I thought it would help me get moving more. (I spend a lot of time in a desk chair.) It did, at first, but then I got used to it and settled back to my sit bones more than I should.

But last week, my soon-to-be stepmom said, "Andi, I'm really hesitant to say this," and she looked my thighs, "but I think you keep putting the care of yourself last. I think you need to take better care of yourself." It was the gentlest, most loving reminder that people care about my health, about the way my body moves and operates. It reminded me that I didn't feel good physically, and that when I don't feel good physically, my emotions tank. And when my emotions tank, my writing suffers.

So I started moving more, and that Fitbit vibrated 10,000 steps on my arm for the last three days. I'm wiped out at the end of each of those days, but in a good way, in a way that tells me I did something useful with my body. Plus, even though today is really busy and full of interruptions and things I had not planned, I don't feel stressed. Somehow the cleaning of our barn and the planting of flowers and the weeding of the garden, all of that has worked some of the stress out from the center of my chest and released it through my limbs.

Today, then, I just want to remind you that part of you is your body. (I don't really buy the body-soul divide thing.) Your body needs to move for your words to move, for your spirits to lift, for your mind to function well. So there's that—my gentle reminder to you to take a walk or lift some weights or do a few sit-ups on the floor of your apartment.

But then there's this, too, a body awareness lets us write better because it reminds us that we and our characters live in bodies. Here are a few ways that awareness is important to me as a writer:

1. **I can write about the physical sensations that accompany my experiences.** For instance, stress reaches my chest and then my shoulders and neck. And glee flutters somewhere around my lungs.

2. **I can use my character's physical experience to enhance not only the description but also the plot of my fiction and essays.** For example, if my girl Mary Steele can't run very fast (and she can't), then I can use that to heighten tension in a scene where she is being chased. Or if I know my mother took comfort in a gentle rubbing of her fingers across her leg (and she did), I can postulate about how this might be linked to the way her piano playing was the time she seemed most fully herself.

3. **I can take my physical description of characters further.** Rather than relying on skin tone, hair color, height, eye color, etc., as the only ways I can paint a physical picture of a character, I can also delve into the way he moves. Is one shoulder higher than the other? Or does one leg not step as broad? (I like to think about asymmetries

for character development.) Or do they clutch at one part of their body when something tragic happens?

Writing Prompt

If you'd like to explore the way physicality can become a richer part of your writing, try this exercise that I learned from the wise and talented Laraine Herring:

Describe your physical body today. Move from head to toe. What feels loose and free? What feels bound up? Then, sink into the freest or tightest places and answer these two questions— what colors do you find in those places? What emotions rest there?

Much love,
Andi

CHAPTER 15

The Angsty Relationship of Writing and Sales

Dear Beautiful People,

Here's what I wish could happen:

1. I write a book or schedule a retreat or offer a service.
2. The world comes storming to my gates to buy, attend, or work with me.

Here's what actually happens:

1. I write a book, schedule a retreat, or offer a service.
2. Crickets have the stage.
3. I decide to promote that book, retreat, or service.
4. I feel angsty and wish I didn't have to promote my work. I do it anyway.
5. A few people unsubscribe or maybe whine about "self-promotion."
6. I feel bad.
7. I keep promoting.

The truth is that I have an uneasy relationship with sales, partially because I really do wish I could just do this work for free, or barter. . . I'm always up for a barter, especially if it involves angora rabbits. But I also have an uneasy relationship with sales because I came to writing through academic means, and academics still live, oddly, with an idea of meritocracy as the way people get recognition for what they do.

In the academic model, you get degrees, you publish articles that (sadly) almost no one reads, and you get a job that you can never lose.

Most of the world does not work this way. In fact, most of the world is not a meritocracy at all . . . it's . . . well, pick your metaphor: battlefield, dog fight, chaotic mass of swirl. For me, I like to see the world as a field of wildflowers. (Stick with me . . . I'm not going to go too hippie dippie.)

My teacher, Sharman Apt Russell, wrote a book called *An Obsession with Butterflies*. (It's a great book, by the way.) She began writing that book with a single question: what does a butterfly see when it enters a meadow full of wildflowers? That image is one that I hold dear because I put myself in the place of the butterfly. I fly into that field, and I see the colors and shapes of all those flowers . . . and I have to choose to start somewhere, right?

The world, then, on my good days, is like that field of wild flowers. We put our books, retreats, services, and courses up and make them as pretty as we can. We choose a color scheme, a petal shape, a height of the stalk, and we set them out in the world for people to see. And we let our flower flag fly. (Love mixing idioms, I do.)

That's all sales is—putting your work out into the world so that people know it's there and can choose it if they want. If they don't want, then they can—and should—say NO. It's not fair to them if we don't give their butterfly selves the choice to see our work, and we can't blame them for not picking our flower if we don't get it out in the field where they can see it.

Now, that's not to say we need to be doing sales all the time or even most of the time. That's like pushing our flower into the beds of our friends' houses. Instead, we share, but in moderation. Here are my three guidelines for sales:

- **25 percent sales; 75 percent helpful stuff that is about other people.** I share other people's content, review their books, post helpful links, share tips, post funny pictures of cows.

- **Sell to the people who care.** I do my best not to flood my general FB or Twitter feeds with sales stuff because the people I know there already know I have books out and can get them when they want. I do post a little in those spaces, but more like 10 percent instead of 25 percent of the time. If you're on this mailing list, then I assume you're most interested in what I have to say about writing, so I share only on that content, and mix in that 25 percent of sales from time to time.

- **Try not to take it personally.** I lost a bunch of folks from this mailing list when I sent a sales email on Monday. That does hurt--I won't lie—but when I get some perspective, I just realize they are not my people. AND I believe firmly that grown-ups should say NO to what they don't want. So I'm glad they're gone . . . mostly. But not in a mean way. You know what I mean, right?

So take this from me . . . it's really okay to promote your own work, even if people tell you it's not. You are proud of what you write, teach, provide. Put it out in the world. Let your flowers rise up toward the sun. Let them glow with pollen . . . and fill us all with delight. (Okay, I'm slipping into hippie dippier love-child land, so I'll stop.)

But really, don't be afraid to sell. Just be responsible and courteous. It's that simple.

Much love,
Andi

CHAPTER 16

So Many Good, Important Things to Do

Hi Beautiful People,

I've been sitting at my computer for twenty minutes now. I knew what I wanted to write to you, felt it important that I say it, and yet, the saying of it is hard today for one simple reason: I'm so very tired.

I'm physically tired, yes, but more I'm mentally tired. For about six weeks now, I've been busy, so, so busy. I've done my best to take down time, and I've—until the past ten days—been diligent about my sleep . . . but I haven't had days when I did normal things in a while . . . days when I wrote and worked in the garden and read and walked and just had a day that was my normal.

So I'm tired, and I'm realizing that this level of tired means I need to look at my life differently, especially since I want to write every day.

Last year, I pared way back on my life, stopped saying yes to too many things and, instead, chose to say no most of the time and yes only to that which gives me joy. It's a privilege to have that option, and it's not one I take for granted.

Now, a year later, on this, the longest day of the year, I'm at another paring point, but this time my choices are harder because I have to choose to pare down things I love. How do I choose between having my garden be rich and sort of weed-free and writing every morning? I'm not sure of the answer yet . . . but I know I'm going to have to make some choices about where I use my time.

So I share that today to say that sometimes we find the time to write by turning off the TV or shutting down Facebook. Sometimes we find it by saying NO to things we don't really want or need to do. And sometimes, we find it by saying NO to things we really love and care about, at least for a time.

I'm not sure what this is going to look like in my life, but I do know it's going to require some major shifts in how I spend my time and in the things I give my best energy to. And I'm okay with that— this fallacy that we're all going to get our lives "balanced" in such a way that they are always going to work that same way is manipulative and deceptive. Life requires constant rebalancing, and I'm just in one of those shifting of the teeter-totter times.

Maybe you're in that place, too. Where you're trying to manage how to be a good partner and a writer, or how to parent well and still find time to write. Or how to do your job that pays your bills and still have energy to get some words down.

If you are, I hope you know that we're all shifting the pieces of life around all the time. There's no magic formula, no one-size-fits-all writer's hat, no "right" way. There's just your way . . . your way for today.

Much love,
Andi

CHAPTER 17

When We Feel Guilty
for Writing

Dear Beautiful People,

Settle in for a second, will you? Turn off the music. Shut down tabs. Close the door behind you. Settle in.

Now, let me ask you something. When do you feel ashamed or guilty for taking time to write? Really, think about the when of that feeling. Is it at a particular time of day? Or when circumstances in your life are a certain way? Is it when the cost in time isn't equaled by the payment in money? Or likes? Or subscriptions?

When do you feel guilt or shame because you take time to do this thing of putting words to the page?

Notice, I didn't ask DO YOU, I asked WHEN DO YOU because almost every writer I know feels guilty or shameful about taking time to write, at least sometimes. I'm not sure why, but this seems to be an integral part of the writing life.

- Some of us feel guilty because we have small children whose demands are many and who—rightly or wrongly—feel we should be attending to them with all of ourselves in every moment, even if blood is not seeping out of skin.

- Some of us feel guilty because we have been conditioned to think that an activity that takes this much effort and time should be compensated financially.
- Some of us feel guilty because people we love say things about "waste" and "something better to do" or "amounting to nothing."
- Some of us feel guilty because we have people in our lives who need our care: our attention, our meal preparation, our bathing hands.
- Some of us feel guilty because we have told ourselves for decades that we aren't any good at this and to do something we aren't good at for so long is irresponsible and selfish.

I don't know if those are your reasons. I have some of most of those most days, but no matter the reason, I hope you can hear me say this:

Writing is not a waste of time. It's not, by nature, selfish. It's not neglectful or navel-gazing.

Writing is also not about making money or accomplishment that is measured beyond ourselves.

Writing is about a way of being, a way of seeing, a way of understanding.

If you are reading this book, you believe—in the way that is right for your life—that writing has value for you. That's enough reason to write, right there.

If you believe writing helps you think better, feel better, be better, understand better, know better, breathe better, then it's not wrong to do it. You are not wasting time or being selfish. You are caring for yourself. And that matters.

It does.

Much love,
Andi

.

CHAPTER 18

Writing Deep Without Over-Reaching

Dear Beautiful People,

This time of year, I usually have swaths of dirt covering my arms and feet . . . evidence of my morning and evening times in the garden. Carrying Swiss chard leaves in to wash, digging potatoes, pulling weeds—they all leave their paintbrush marks of work on my skin . . . and I love it.

For me, gardening is deep work. It takes all my concentration and all my body's focus to do it well, even though I know mostly what I'm doing when I prep the soil, plant the seeds, and tend the beds. Even the rote requires profound concentration . . . and for that reason, tending a garden is a great gift to my soul.

Writing is that, too, when I allow myself to go deep with it. . . when I put all of my concentration into the work, I am tugged down into a world beneath the surface where mystical creatures that I have imagined but don't yet exist swim and breathe. Sometimes these creatures are new people, sometimes the faces of the wounds carved into my spirit. Sometimes they are flippered things or witch's brooms or the call of a tiny, tiny hummingbird that I didn't know I knew how to hear.

All of them—in their truest, richest form—live beneath the surface, and I have to go very deep to find them. Deeper than I often allow myself to go.

The Surface of the Mind

We all know it when we read it: the work of someone who has tried too hard, overworked an idea, pushed too much toward the clever. We sense a falseness there, a taint of insincerity . . . it's harder to sense that "offness" in our own writing, though . . . at least it is for me.

I have learned, though, if the physical sensation of writing seems to be in my head. If I'm squinting or clenching my jaw, if my mind's eye-view is taking me into my brain, I'm probably trying very hard to find the deep on the surface.

The mind is not the playground of the deep. The heart is.

The longer I write, the more I'm certain this is the case. We need to know things; we need research to make our writing rich and accurate. But for it to be powerful, authentic, for it to do that magical thing that books do when they wrap us in their spell, writing has to be heart-work, not headwork.

How I Get Past My Head into My Heart

I am terrible at this. Profoundly terrible. Monkey mind has built a jungle palace in my skull, and King Louis dances a polka in my brain most days. My thoughts move so fast. My to-do list spins a whirl. My memories slide in and out like curtains.

But I have learned—sometimes—to get past all that and settle into the seat I imagine in the center of my chest. (Yours may be behind your left hip or tucked in the folds of your belly button. But it's there somewhere in the torso of your body . . . maybe spend some time thinking about where.)

Here are five things I do to settle in and go deep into myself.

1. **I shut things down or don't open them at all.** Most days, I have at least three tabs, a notebook, and some notes open around me. To write deep, I have to shut all those and put them away. I can't see notifications or look at my to-do list. It all has to be closed down. Or if I'm really working well, like it feels I am today, I don't open anything at all before I write.

2. **I take deep breaths.** When I breathe deep, I feel, as a yoga instructor used to tell me, my lungs open out like wings. I find the space that I imagine the Holy Spirit moves within me, the breath on the waters. I slow my mind by concentrating on my breathing. I sit for as long as it takes for me to feel my jaw relax. For me, that's the physical marker.

3. **I visualize going behind and below.** I'm not sure I have the language to quite capture this yet, but when I'm writing deep, I'm not picturing what is happening on the page. Instead, I'm imagining that I, my mind, my words—I'm not sure—are stepping behind things or swimming below them. It's like I'm trying to get as far backstage as I can so I can watch the action from the most removed angle. When I go to this place, it's like I'm looking at my memories, for instance, from below. The irony of this place is that though I've removed the emotional resonance I feel with what I'm witnessing is profound.

4. **I resist the temptation to step away.** I once heard fiction writer Ron Carlson say that the trick to good writing was to stay at the desk when you wanted to get that second cup of coffee. For me, the key is to resist the temptation to check Facebook or email . . . and sometimes get more

coffee. When I'm inclined to look away, I know—finally—
that it's that moment when I need to dive in, not come up
for air.

5. **I let my body show me what I may not yet
    know.** Sometimes, I am writing, and I feel my throat pull
    tight and my face crumple as tears pour forth. Sometimes,
    I feel my belly ache or my chest constrict. Sometimes, my
    feet just need to bounce. When that happens, I latch on to
    my body and follow it because the body carries things the
    mind has not yet understood—profound grief, anger
    locked up, sorrow long forgotten. So to go as deep as
    possible, I attend to my physical presence, let her take my
    hand, and follow her into the depths.

You may need to wrap other language around these practices of
going deep—take words that come more from your cultural or faith
tradition—and that's exactly what you need to do. Make this your
own and then see where it goes.

If you'd like to read more about some of these ideas, check out
Laraine Herring's book *Writing Begins with the Breath* and Gayle
Brandeis' *Fruitflesh*. (Men, Gayle's book looks like it's just for
women, but you'll find goodness there, too.)

If I could offer one more thing for you to carry away with you, I
want to say that we don't need your cleverness or your fancy
language. We need you. So go deep, my friends.

Much love,
Andi

CHAPTER 19

Giving Space

Dear Beautiful People,

If you would, close your eyes and imagine the most beautiful thing you've ever experienced. Let it pull you close . . . see the colors, hear the movement stilled for a split second, and lean into the void of nothing around the color or sound you experience. What I want you to feel, my friends, is the emptiness there. Let it tug at you, pull you in.

Now, sit where you are in this moment. Turn down the music. Dim the lights if you can. Walk outside or into a closet to quiet if you need. Feel the nothingness that is most of the space around you . . . then feel deeper, feel the energy there. Take a deep breath. And another. And another.

I've been taking a lot of deep breaths lately. This morning, I went out to the garden to harvest, as I do each morning this time of year. Usually, I put in earbuds and listen to a podcast or book, but this morning, I went out bare with the gentle intention of holding space for whatever I needed to hear or see.

I picked cucumbers and then started to walk by the asparagus beans, taking note that they had their purple blossom dresses on. But then, I slowed and bent nearer . . . and there were beans, three-foot long beauties that had been there for days—days when I had walked past this trellis fifty times. But each time, I had been so busy doing whatever it was I thought needed me that I had missed them . . .

I spent the next minutes twisting the bean vines up onto the trellis with gentle twirls so that I wouldn't miss the beans again.

Here's what I take from those few moments: I have to hold space to be surprised. I have to hold space to see the fruits of what I've done. I have to hold space for my words to find new climbing trellises. **I have to hold space wide open and take the gifts that are given.**

Maybe you are much better at this than I am, but if you're not, try this week to hold space for two things:

1. **Hold space for nothing.** Intentionally create short periods (or long periods if you have them) of time where you just wander or sit on the porch and stare or look out the window at the rain. Notice what you think about, what your mind feels like, how your breath slows.

2. **Hold space for your words.** Writing is not something that happens spontaneously, at least not in my experience. We have to be creating space for it, space to think, space to let ideas percolate, space for the actual manifestations of language to be noticed, and space for the physical act of extracting those words and writing them down.

So this week, my friends, try slowing down. Stare at beautiful things. Listen to music without doing anything else. Read a book for three hours in a row if you can. Give yourself space so that your words can breathe, too.

Much love,
Andi

CHAPTER 23

The Best Thing I've Done for My Writing Life

Dear Beautiful People,

Eight years ago, I quit my full-time job as a college English professor. It was absolutely the right thing to do . . . particularly because it made me take my work as a writer seriously. Now, I had to buy my groceries through that work. Suddenly, I couldn't play at writing—I had to take it seriously.

And I did take it seriously for all of those eight years, but in the past year—as my business has grown and as our farm business has become to live on its own—I've begun to really buckle down and think about writing as a way of following the course of our life and our dreams. It is our primary source of income now, and it continues to grow.

What that means for me as a writer is that I can't afford to procrastinate. I can't afford to give in to the unease I feel about marketing. I can't afford to devalue my work and underprice my services. I work hard writing, editing, coaching, and marketing for the full value of the services I provide or someone goes hungry.

This reality has been the BEST THING for my writing life.

Now, I don't flake when I have an opportunity to publish something in a place that pays or gives me good exposure (and I mean GOOD exposure, not just piddly exposure). I don't skip a blog post or an email to this community or a day of posting in my FB groups because—in addition to loving all of you, and I REALLY do—I have a commitment to all of you that is directly tied into the success of my business. I don't give away my work unless there's a strategy behind FREE that builds my business. I don't put off writing my books.

The result is that I'm better at my job than I was when I wrote for free, when I didn't take my blog seriously, and when I was always afraid to charge what I'm worth. I'm WAY better because I know that my family's livelihood depends on my work . . .

Here's what I've discovered: when I honor that my writing is actual work, when I charge for it and schedule it, when I turn down clients because they cannot pay my rates, when I hold the prices steady for the things I offer, and when I eschew the still-rising guilt that says I'm not worth it—people respect what I do more, for one, AND I'm able to offer important, valuable services for FREE without putting my family, our farm, or even my dreams and self-esteem on precarious footing.

Now, I don't think financial worth is the measure of writing worth . . . not at all. But I do think culturally, we prioritize things that pay, and so it can be a helpful exercise to consider our writing as if we are paid for it, even if we're not, so that we can give it some level of priority in our days.

So here's my challenge for you today: what if you took your writing as seriously as you do the job that pays your bills? What would that change about your writing life?

Much love,
Andi

P.S. I don't recommend quitting your job to write unless you have other sources of income on hand. I tutored online and adjuncted until my dad paid my bill for eighteen months. He's the best dad.

CHAPTER 20

The Waiting

Dear Beautiful People,

Sometimes, all of life feels like a wait . . . that's not just me, right? We wait for answers, or change, for that call. We wait for a response from a publisher or that feedback from our first readers or those edits. Sometimes, there is nothing to do but wait.

I find that to be one of the hardest things in life. I am a doer. I like to make things happen. I like to learn and try and go. I like to be in control.

And yet, so much of life is not able to be controlled. So much of writing, too.

I am learning that, learning to sit back and wait . . . to keep doing that which calls for me in the daily—the daily writing, the reading, the sharing—AND to not keep adding in things to do just because I'm waiting. The waiting time does not need to be filled.

In the past month, I have done four jigsaw puzzles. They are the way I am choosing to take breaks just now. When I read much of late, I find myself distracted by my thoughts . . . waiting for me often comes at a time when I really need to process, not do, or I fall asleep.

So jigsaw puzzles let me think while giving me something else to focus on so I don't obsess or over-research or fill my time with too much input.

Last night I sang while I finished one. I cried a little, too. It was perfect.

Here, then, is Ted Kooser's wisdom for writers. Write. Wait. Revisit. That may be good life advice, too. There is a way of seeing that comes when we sit with the openness of a waiting space, a new set of eyes, a distance that gives us more openness about what we've created . . . or what we've been handed if we're talking about life.

So my friends, take in the waiting times if you can. Create new things while you wait AND leave space for the jigsaw puzzle moments where things might not fall into place, but maybe you will.

Much love,
Andi

CHAPTER 21

Listening and Letting Go

Dear Beautiful People,

Last week, I finished re-reading Madeleine L'Engle's book *Walking on Water*, and since then, I have been thinking about how much of writing is about understanding who we are as writers, how much about listening to the work, and how much about letting go. I'm struck, thus, with the fact that when the writing goes well, when it feels its richest and most true somehow, it's when I've most gotten out of the way of myself.

Let me see if I can explain through a story.

Just about this time last year, Philip and I flew to Alaska to spend two weeks with my dad, brother, and sister-in-law. It was the final promise that Dad had made to Mom: he would return to Alaska, and we all joined him in that journey. We had an amazing time together—the Alaska landscape is absolutely soul-stunning—and then, everyone else flew home while Dad and I drove back. He had

65

driven up by himself and didn't really relish the idea of a drive home alone.

The first day, we drove fourteen hours, out of Anchorage over the Chugach Mountains and down into the Yukon Territory of Canada. For over two hours we saw no other cars and no other signs of human habitation as we made our way across the northern parts of our home continent. We finally made it to a hotel on a first nations' reservation and found ourselves able to rent a log cabin at half-price for the night. We scarfed a burger in the closing cafe and headed for bed.

At 4:00 a.m., I heard Dad in the shower. He couldn't sleep, and then I couldn't get back to sleep. So we hit the road. I was exhausted and wanted to enjoy that cabin, but Dad needed to keep moving. So I got in the driver's seat, backed away from the river on which the cabin sat and which we had not seen in daylight, and headed east.

We were on a very open, very empty stretch of road when I saw them. Dancing streams of light in the sky. I pulled the van over, and Dad and I stood on the side of a Yukon highway watching the Northern Lights put on their show. They were mystical, magical, almost normal in the way the most precious things are. We stood for a long time and watched them move.

Now, here's the thing—I had spent our entire trip hoping to see the Northern Lights, but conditions weren't favorable. I had hoped to check that item off my very short bucket list, and it hadn't looked like it was going to happen.

Then it did because I did what I needed to do—to be with my dad when he needed me, to attend to his anxiety to be on the road home, to drive across openness for hours the day before because we had no choice—and to be here, on a prairie, to watch the magic.

Writing is the same, I think. We put ourselves where we need to be: even when we're tired, even when we don't feel like it, and then we keep our eyes and ears open for the dance.

This, then, is my challenge and prayer and hope for each of you:

May you put yourself where you can see the magic on the page. May you trust it will be there, even if you don't see it. May you let yourself listen and may you let yourself dance.

Much love,
Andi

CHAPTER 22

Embrace the Mystery

Dear Beautiful People,

I debated about writing on the importance of having a ripple-like wave of action/tension/conflict in prose, and I've thought about writing some about balancing the business side of writing with the creative side, but now, on this perfect early fall afternoon when Paco, our neighbor donkey, has just brayed to call out an entire crew of dogs and goats over to hang out, I feel like writing about mystery is more fitting.

Also, I just woke up from one of those naps where I am thinking through a joy-filled fog, so embracing the between seems wise.

Living the Questions

Rilke's *Letters to a Young Poet* is one of those books I keep near me always. I can remember the first time I read it. I was in my early twenties and in a coffee shop in Richmond. My then boyfriend was probably in a guitar store nearby. I had a pen, and I underlined most of the book. I can see what I saw out the cafe door, the parking lot of the bakery where my brother would get his wedding cake in the months to come.

The book was that important. Years later, when that boyfriend-turned-husband and just weeks from being ex-husband and I moved back East from San Francisco, my pastor and dear friend, Theresa, would give me a card with Rilke's words on it, and I would hang that card in my first professorial office. It would hang there until I left three years later.

The lines I underlined and Theresa quoted, the ones I hold close to myself when all the mysteries are so vast are these:

> I beg you, to have patience with everything unresolved in your heart and to try to love the questions themselves as if they were locked rooms or books written in a very foreign language. Don't search for the answers, which could not be given to you now because you would not be able to live them. And the point is to live everything. Live the questions now. Perhaps then, someday far in the future, you will gradually, without even noticing it, live your way into the answer.

I hold these words for living . . . and for writing.

I believe with everything I have as a writer that the best work we do is when we lean into the mystery. We write into what compels us without reason, into the pains we don't yet understand, into the questions that come again and again. The mysteries, my friends, that's where the energy is.

What Makes You Angry

In those three years when I was teaching college students full time, I had the honor of designing the college's first creative writing class, and one of the first assignments I gave them on one of the first days was this:

Write about something that feels trivial but really makes you angry.

My example to them was that I get unreasonably peeved when posters are left up after an event's date has passed. I encouraged them to write into that small mystery, to explore the tension between what they knew they should just get over and the fact that they could not get over it. Some of the best essays, poems, and stories came from that question.

Ask the Fruitful Questions

In grad school, back when that man was the husband who had not yet decided to leave, I took a seminar with the amazing YA and nature writer, Sharman Apt Russell. In that course, she talked about asking fruitful questions—I've mentioned this before, I know; it was that monumental in shaping me as a writer—the questions that require you to learn to answer them, the ones that make you research and go deep and think laterally.

Her seminar taught me so much about letting go of control, about leaning into what I didn't know, what I didn't understand. In many ways, that one seminar has shaped every aspect of who I am as a writer.

Because here's the one thing I have figured out: if I know what something means, if I know its deepest significance, if I already understand something, then the energy to write it is already dissipated. I've already burned it up, and when I write, it will droop like a plant without water . . . and I won't even have the pleasure of the dried-up and crackling leaf.

This is, perhaps, one of the reasons I am a "pantser" in writing because I like to leave as much mystery as possible. But even if you are a "planner," an outliner, someone who thrives on having the general direction of a piece laid out, I urge you to leave room for mystery, for turns down alleys and woodland trails that you did not expect. I encourage you to listen to the characters that are coming to life before you and let them give you directions. I hope you will let the word play of those sounds in that stanza draw you deep into the well that echoes your voice into new things.

Embrace the mystery, friends. Let the hailing echo of a donkey call you to the story in ways you never imagined.

Much love,
Andi

CHAPTER 24

Resting on the Discipline

Dear Beautiful People,

Just now, here at the end of a busy but not frantic day, the silence of my house is broad. It comes into the caves of my ears and rings. This time of day (just before 4:00 p.m.) is special to me. It's the sacred time of coming home, the one I had for years of school buses and classrooms, the one now of the pick-up truck down the driveway after it stops for the mail.

It amazes me how much space just my own thoughts can fill, the noise they can make.

My eyes fill with the gift of the silence and the school bus going by.

It's been a long day filled with the work that must be done.

Part of me wants to eschew work, to become fully engrossed in art, as I imagine the romantics were. Wordsworth taking long walks along the lakes. Coleridge with his feet propped on the arm of a sofa as he reclines.

I forget that sometimes these men went without food.

In one of the earliest images I have of my father, he is carrying a railroad tie, the base of it resting in his clasped fingers, across our driveway. He was building a railroad tie wall around our parking area, holding back the red clay of the North Carolina mountains. He didn't have any help.

It took him ten years, but when we moved, that hillside was the most glorious rock garden I've ever seen. Trails laid with mulch and lined with split rails, a rail fence around the perimeter, multi-stem birch that I stood in like a young go-go dancer, glee my outfit and my energy.

The same is true of his house at Bremo, my home, the way it went from bare-cut clay and grass to shade and columbine and a pond with at least a dozen frogs.

I look here, at the garden new and the barn and the shape that is coming to the space where we remember the people enslaved here, and it feels too slow and already so fast.

It is the work of silences and seasons, this building of gardens.

On the days when running my own businesses and writing my own pages feels too hard, I dream of the days when I worked in a bookstore, where the task at hand was simply to fill my hours with what came to mesa bin of books to sort into the alphabet and fit onto shelves, customers who strolled up with one title or a basket full, the reshelving of titles discarded.

I could spend hours there, enrapt in other people's words and in ordering them by rules arbitrary to what was said.

Someday, I will go back to that work.

Today, I am tired, and I've been told I must avoid all stress. I have a long list of all that there is to do, and I have a book of revisions to finish. We have bills due at the beginning-end of the month, and I am writing books to make $2, $3 at a time.

Still, I wake far before light, and I spend time with Word and words. Then, I flip to Chapter 11, count the number of pages in the chapter, and pick up a pen.

Sometimes, it's the discipline of the practice, the showing up every day until it becomes simply what you do, like a single man carrying a full railroad tie alone.

Sometimes, then, you sit at the end of the day and let the silence ring into the spaces between your ribs, and you are grateful for soft hands and for the way you can sit at your own window and watch the school bus pass by.

Much love,
Andi

P.S. I hope you are carving out a practice, a habit of writing that works for you so that on the heavy, hard days when you don't feel like it, writing is still what you do because it is, simply, what you have done.

CHAPTER 25

Sometimes, Writers, We Need Help

Dear Beautiful People,

Right now, I am in Denver, Colorado, visiting one of my dearest friends and her family. Philip and I had been wanting to come visit, but it's on the generosity of our friends, who used their airline miles to get our plane tickets, that made this trip possible for us. We couldn't have afforded it otherwise.

This, my friends, is hard for me. I don't like to be a burden on people. I have a hard time taking gifts, even ones freely given, but I am learning to do so . . . especially as a writer.

Literary Citizenship

I believe very mightily in the importance of literary citizenship. As writers, we need to operate as part of a community that supports, promotes, challenges, and leans into one another. The experience of writing itself is a solitary one, but the work around that writing, well, that's group work in every way.

We need each other to read our books and review our books. We need folks to share our blogs and leave comments. We need people to pick us up when that mean-spirited comment brings us down. We need to have folks who will tell us to "keep going" when we're in those days where we are pretty sure everything we are writing is trash and should be burned like a pile of autumn leaves.

I try to do these things for as many people as I can, and I've finally learned that it's okay to ask people to help me, too.

How to Ask for Help

If you are at all like me, it can be a very hard thing to ask people for help, especially with something as personal and risky as writing. I want to hunker down and just do it myself . . . but it doesn't work that way. We need each other.

So here are a few things I do to be sure I have earned the right to ask for help from other writers and readers:

- **I try to give at least three times as often as I ask.** I write reviews. I post photos of other author's books. I share blog posts that resonate with me or that might resonate with others. I run a free online writing community to help support writers with encouragement and accountability. I write newsletter articles and blog posts that, I hope, are helpful to the people who read them. I serve on book launch teams as much as I'm able. Before I even think of asking others, I offer help first.

- **I am specific about what will help.** If I need reviews over on Kobo, I ask for them. If I want to hit a certain sales goal, I let people know. If I'm feeling discouraged or beaten down by comments, I go to a few writer friends and let them know what I need to be reminded of. It's not helpful to just say, "Help me" if the people who love you don't know how.

- **I say thank you early and often.** I thank people who review my work, who share it. I like tweets and FB posts anytime I'm mentioned and, if appropriate, thank the writer, too. I post public thank yous, and I write thank you notes. A heartfelt thank-you lets people know you noticed their work on your behalf and shows appreciation in just the smallest way for their time and effort. It's essential.

When People Criticize Us for Asking

Inevitably, if you are asking for help, especially in a culture like America's, where independence is seen as the highest virtue, you will likely be criticized and critiqued for being "needy" or "self-promoting."

Here's how I handle that: **I acknowledge that it's true. Then, I think about how sad it is when people feel like they can't acknowledge their needs and reach out to others.**

There is no shame in asking for help. (Can you hear me repeating that to myself over and over?) We all need help. Sometimes, though, people are harder on artists who ask than they are on say, the cookie company that advertises four hundred times a day on TV because art is considered a "lesser" form of work by many.

But we can't own that. We need to do our work, ask for the help we need, and give the help we can.

Break through the Shame Wall

Be brave, my friends. Ask for people to review your books or read your blogs. Suggest your titles to friends who need gifts for others. Email book club leaders and ask if they'd like you to come talk to their group about your book.

Because here's the thing: you are offering something to the world with your work. Your book, your blog, your article, your lyrics, your poem—those are gifts you are giving. There's no shame in wanting people to have your gift . . . there's only love there.

So ask . . . and start now.

Much love,
Andi

CHAPTER 26

Push Through or Step Back?

Dear Beautiful People,

It has been a BUSY month. A trip. My husband's birthday. A book launch. A craft show on the farm. Family in town. Finishing a second book in two months. I'm tired . . . good tired. But tired.

BUT I have a new book coming out in three weeks. (More details below.) And I am launching two courses in early 2017. And I have clients to serve. I still have a lot to do.

So here's the question I'm weighing each day - when do I need to push through, and when do I need to take a break?

Pushing Through

Here's how I decide what I need to push through on:

- Is it about the necessities of life, for people I love, or for our animals?
- Is it about a deadline that must be met for myself or for a client?

- Is it about something discrete and short-lived that I will be glad to have done and that will not be followed by twenty-five other tasks that are the same in nature?

If those criteria are met, then I keep going.

Taking a Break

Here's how I decide when I need to take a break:

- Have I done a good day's work?
- Have I finished what must be done for a day, AND is my criteria for "must be done" reasonable?
- Am I resentful when someone asks for something, or do I dread doing things that I typically enjoy?

If the answer to any of those things is "yes," then I need to take a break. For me, that final question is the big one.

The Grumpy/Weepy Test

The ultimate indicator of when I need to take a break is this: if I resent having to do something for someone, if I get weepy at simple things like having to load the dishwasher or cry over sappy TV commercials, if I hear a tone in my voice that I associate with one certain, bitter English teacher I had, I need to take a break.

As a quintessential introvert, the best thing I can do then is to shut down alone for a few hours. I typically sew and watch TV shows I love. Then, within four hours or so, I feel much better.

I did this yesterday, so you're welcome. You don't need that English-teacher tone in a newsletter.

The Writing Test

It's much trickier for me to determine when to work and when to rest in terms of a writing project. Since writing is one of the things that helps keep me healthy, sometimes I NEED to write when I'm tired.

So I have to come up with a couple other criteria to help me determine if I need to take a break from a particular piece of work. I ask myself these questions:

- Am I really stuck here, or is this a place where I need to go deeper instead of stepping away?
- Is fear dictating my choice? If it is, then I need to stay.

Then, I determine two things:

- **For how long am I going to be away?** Usually a fifteen-minute break will do it for me on most days. If I need an extended break, I try not to be away from a work in progress, i.e., a draft in progress, for more than a week. Any longer than that, and I can't remember what I was doing.
- **What will I do during my break?** The best thing I can do is something like work on a jigsaw puzzle or color, or maybe take a walk. I can't check Facebook or begin something complex because I'll get pulled away for too long.

Then, I come back and go back in.

This Is Counter-Cultural

Almost everything in our culture says we should "soldier on" and "power through." We hear messages about "toughening up" and "aim higher" all the time . . . and if you're like me, those messages shout VERY LOUDLY when it comes to my writing life.

But here's the fundamental thing I have to remember. Writing is an act of creativity, and creativity is unbounded and radical. It needs space to be able to spin itself out, and if we are always "powering through" and "soldiering on," we are filling all the space in our lives. Writing needs air around it, and writers need to take deep breaths.

Sometimes breathing requires that we take a break, and there is not a bit of shame in that.

So friends, if you feel overwhelmed and like you're just holding on to get to the end of the day, if your writing projects and platform building and blogging and all the rest of your life make it feel like you can never slow down, hear me when I say that I know just what you mean AND it's important to slow down, especially when it seems like you can't. There's no shame in needing a break or just wanting one. In fact, you may be doing yourself and your writing the best favor you can.

Breathe deep, my friends.

Much love,
Andi

A Writer's Greatest Strength

Dear Beautiful People,

Late in my new book, *Charlotte and the Twelve,* Charlotte is telling the people gathered in the school where she once taught what she wants from those gathered. She begins this way:

"Listen." Charlotte's one word brought all our righteous fidgeting to a halt. She looked each of us in the eye. "We are going to listen."

I wrote that scene in one of those gentle spaces that signals I have reached the center of the writing world, the world I think of as a forest. The scene came through very differently than I had thought it would, which is, of course, a sure sign that it is truer and righter than anything I could have created. For me, this scene is the crux of the novel. It speaks the loudest truth in those pages . . . and I cannot take credit for it but by saying I was a way.

I wrote those pages because I was listening to the story, to the characters, to the lesson this book needed to teach me.

A Writer's Greatest Strength

I know, with all that I am, that my greatest work as a writer comes when I listen, when I listen well. Whether it's to my characters, to the story, to the experiences and reading I've done, to other people in my life, to the voices of people I don't know and will never meet . . . when I am turned on to the deepest way of writing, I am listening. It is my greatest strength.

When we listen as writers, we put aside our own agendas. We shut away our need to be heard. We turn down the quest for affirmation that often drives us. And instead, we open ourselves up. We stop driving forward. We become still. We let the stories in.

I have a lot of opinions, a lot of perspectives, a lot of arguments I want to win. But I've learned—by trial and error and by witness—that pushing an agenda, teaching a lesson, endowing my will on people, even in story, is the quickest way to turn off readers and lose sight of the truth.

But when I let the space within my imagination's ears grow wide, when I slow my breath and unclench my jaw, when I tune in for real, I can hear truth that lives behind words, truth that shadows them and lights them up, truth that speaks of the core reality of this world: that we are all broken, that we are all loved.

Five Ways I Help Cultivate a Spirit of Listening in Myself

I am not good at this. I like to win arguments and decimate flimsy points of view. I like to drive an idea home with an arrow-like ferocity. I like to silence other people so I can be heard. So when I share these things, I share them because I have NEEDED—for my writing and for my heart—to find them.

1. I keep empty space in my day. At the beginning of the day, in the late afternoon, and before I go to sleep, I

make sure I have a few minutes without a device, without an audio book, without anything else playing for me to take in, and I sit and ponder what I've heard—both from outside myself and from within myself—today. This space lets me pinpoint discomfort, ponder a person's intention, and go deep with the stories that I'm contemplating.

2. **I wait before I respond.** This one is the hardest for me. I think fast, and I want to respond fast. But whether it's to something online, to an idea I have for a book, to something I read, I am learning that I need to take time to let something settle into me before I speak. I hear better that way.

3. **I take a posture of listening.** My friend Nancy reminded me of the importance of facing someone with our whole bodies when we are listening to them, the way our posture can telegraph inattention, defensiveness, or antagonism. And it's not only in face-to-face conversation. The same is true online.

4. **I pay attention to my body.** When something bothers me, confuses me, angers me, or inspires me, the first place I know is in my body. I can feel myself flush or get tingly, but if I don't slow down and attend that feeling, I miss it entirely sometimes. That's especially true for me when I write. Sometimes, the best things I write make me feel as if a window of light has opened in my chest. I have to be listening to know that.

5. **I go deep.** Often, the things I most need to hear are behind what is right on the surface. Sometimes, my own voice is shouting so loudly that I can't hear anything else. So I imagine myself going deep into a pocket of silence, and I turn my listening inward and

see what whispers to me. It's almost always something hard but beautiful.

When Charlotte whispered "Listen," as I wrote those pages, she was reminding me of what I most need to be the empathetic, wide-minded, compassionate writer I wanted to be. I thank her for that gift.

Much love,
Andi

CHAPTER 27

Some Writerly Love from Me to You

Dear Beautiful People,

This morning, I was reading, thinking, praying in the way that those things all wrap together for me. I was trying to decide what I wanted to write in this newsletter—some tips on writing scene maybe or just a general Happy Holidays—**but then it occurred to me that what I most needed to hear most days is that I am loved, just as I am, right now, weaknesses, failures, flaws, and all.**

And I thought maybe you needed to hear that, too. So today, let me tell you that you are loved for all of who you are. With your beauties and your blemishes. For the areas in which you excel and those in which you fumble. In every success you have and in every heart-breaking failure. You are loved.

Whether you are just starting out on this writing journey or have ten books in the world, whether you believe you are a writer or doubt that every hour, you are loved . . . and **because you are loved, your words, your writing matters.**

So let this be my gift to you. If it helps, write it on a card that you see when you open the cabinet for a cereal bowl or slid back the medicine cabinet for the meds that keep you alive. **You, my beautiful, broken friend are loved deeply and madly every minute of every day.**

May your holidays be bright, even if they are sorrowful. May you find time with friends and family uplifting or may you find the strength and laughter you need when they are not. May you find the space to see your own shining heart and to hear your deepest, truest voice.

Much love,
Andi

CHAPTER 28

Looking on Ourselves and Our Work with True Love

Dear Beautiful People,

When one is being frugal, cannot stream video, and has a lot of crocheting to do, one watches a lot of holiday movies. Thus, I have seen probably ten formulaic, Christmas-themed films in the last week, and therefore, I sort of have gushy, swooshy romance on the brain.

But it's not this super-sweet love that I think is the most powerful thing. Rather, the kind of love that really changes the world is the love that isn't blinding by the first blush of romance and endorphins. Rather, it's the love that hunkers down, that sees the flaws in the other person and that chooses to love them anyway. It's the gray between the black and white of love or hate. It's the between way that is the strongest, most powerful.

This love works powerfully for writers, too. When we can look at our work and see all its beauty and potential AND all the things we need to improve. Our writing allows us to improve it, unlike our partners, friends, or family, and thus, it is, by far, easier than human relationships.

If we really love our work, if we really want it to be as powerful and broad-reaching as we dream it will be, we need to stick with it even when it seems horrible, and we need to mold it even when it seems awesome.

It can be easy to see our work as only with the eyes of that rosy, first blush that comes when we finish it, but if we cannot see past the romance of our words, we cannot make it more of what it needs it to be.

Likewise, we can easily see our work as only its flaws and forget what drew us into it during those first days. When we see with only the bitter hew of negativity, we can find it too easy to walk away from something, deciding it's not worth it and leaving it unfinished and unfettered in the world.

But when we can sink into the deep trenches of love with our work, when we are willing to traverse the shadows and look for the beauty in the crevices, well, then, our work can really shine.

So as we move into these holi-days, hold your work with both scrutiny and rapt attention . . . and hold yourselves that way, too . . . for to love your work, I truly believe you have to love the one who creates it.

Much love and Happy Holidays to you,
Andi

CHAPTER 30

Go Small and Go Gentle

Dear Beautiful People,

Today is the last day that my office will be the couch. Tomorrow, I'm moving back to my actual office, at least for mornings, and using the beautiful standing desk Philip built me for Christmas. I must admit that this return to a more rigorous work schedule has got me a little anxious. I've really needed this past month to be slower and slow down, and I wish I had more of that time.

But I also know that too much slowness means atrophy and apathy, so tomorrow, back I go.

I have a tendency to overshoot restarts. I want to begin with huge goals and feel like I'm starting with a sense of accomplishment. But when I do that, I go the way of most New Year's resolvers and find that I'm burnt, disillusioned, and disappointed right away.

So this year, I'm going small. I'm setting really gentle intentions—intentions marked by boundaries—for my writing life. Here are the three daily things I'm intending:

- Writing/researching from 7:30 a.m. to 9:00 a.m. In that time, I want to go back to my 1,000 words and move forward on some research for a new creative nonfiction book. I'm simply holding that space for my writing.
- Disconnecting from the internet for most of the day. I'll be offline from 7:30 a.m. until 3:00 p.m., if I can. But I'll be gentle with myself here, too, maybe giving myself a lunchtime check-in, too.
- Reading more for pleasure. I have a goal to read two books a week simply because I want to. I plan on donning headphones during chores, so I can listen, and I want to turn to books instead of TV more often.

Maybe you want to send some gentle intentions for your writing and reading practice? If so, I encourage you to go smaller with the idea that you can go bigger if you want. It's easier to build momentum than start over.

Much love,
Andi

CHAPTER 31

Look for the Intersections

Dear Beautiful People,

Twenty years ago, I was sitting in the library at college and working on a paper about Angela Carter, that mistress of post-modern fairy tales. I can't for the life of me remember anything about that paper except that it had the word "mosaic" in the title.

I had been seeing mosaics everywhere, noticing the actual pieces of art, thinking about the way broken things get made into new things, pondering the mosaic that was my own, young life.

And there, with all the blonde wood of study tables and the metal scaffolding of bookshelves around me, **I had what would turn out to be the biggest epiphany I have had to date about writing: the energy for the best writing subjects and forays comes from the places where the intersections are impossible to ignore.**

Let me see if I can give an example. Right now, I am in the beginning stages of research about the people who were enslaved here on our farm. That research means I need to know about the

Berry family who built this place and who enslaved these individuals. I've started constructing the Berry family tree, and I've been reading all I can about the Berry family members. Then, last week, I went to my regular knitting-crochet group, and my friend Bonny mentioned the Berrys she knew, and later that night, another woman talked about so-and-so Berry, who she saw at the river. Then, I saw Berry on a tombstone at the cemetery Philip and I visited on Saturday, and then I noticed it on a mailbox on the way home. There's a lineup of intersections happening here.

Surely there is some magic at work there, absolutely, the magic of life and spiderweb entanglements, yes. But there is also this— **I am at work, and so my eyes are open to see what is before me.** If I wasn't actively putting my mind to this research, if I wasn't carrying the questions pretty close to the surface of my mind most of the time now, I wouldn't see these intersections, the way these threads weave.

So here's my gentle pressure for you today: be at the work and then keep your eyes open. You never know just what might intersect with your path.

Much love,
Andi

CHAPTER 32

Heart Song

Dear Beautiful Writers,

One of my favorite things in the world is when someone comes to tell me a story and is so overwhelmed with the desire to tell that they can't get it out. Sometimes, emotion or enthusiasm make it hard for them to get the words out, and I stand and wait with anticipation, the energy in my fingers beginning to tingle.

Sadly, by the time we are adults, this frenetic need to share is often gone, worn out of us by responsibility and decorum, a misshaped sense of our importance, or by voices that have told us our stories aren't worth telling. So mostly, I hear this energy in young children, when they come running up and say, "Andi, Andi, guess what happened? First . . . and then, and then, and then . . ." They are so caught up in the desire to share that the power of the telling overwhelms the story itself.

Maybe this is the way we all—in an unbroken world—will feel about stories. I certainly hope so.

Heart Work, Not Head Work

If you've hanging around my words very long, you've probably heard me say that I believe writing to be heart work, not head work. With all of who I am, I believe that the truest things we do come straight from the deep parts of ourselves, from the center of our chests where the orange-gold light glows, rather than from the cold, gray, winding matter of our brains.

I suspect there's more than just a wise design for safety at play in the fact that our hearts are buried deep behind bone and muscle, lung and spine. They are protected, and they are central. Anatomically and metaphorically, the heart is located where it can reach out to all the rest of us and fuel us forward.

So when I want to go real, when I ache to reach that place where my writing flows like breathing, I turn myself toward my center and fall in. (I so wish I had better words for this, but maybe, this falling is beyond words, and maybe there is grace in that.) There, in that space, I feel the unbound energy of "and then, and then, and then" that I hear in those tiny voices of child storytellers, and I let it wash over me.

But when I'm out of balance, when I am too committed to what I think is the right thing to say or too worried about what other people will say, or too focused on figuring it out, I stay in the cool, upper space of my mind. There, I find my words dampered and dampened, detached and cutting. In my headspace, the voices that speak ugly to me are so loud that sometimes they shout me down to silence.

So I try—or maybe really what I do is give up trying—and let myself slide down into that orange-gold glow of my heart, the place where story lives.

Writing from YOUR Heart

I don't know just what will let you slip more easily out of your head and into your heart when you write. For me, a candle, quiet, limited distractions, and a turning of my inward eyes down and in usually works, but here are a few things to try:

Play the music you love. Play it to the volume where it fills you. Dance a little. Sing along. Let the rhythm move you. (Come on, you know Gloria Estefan was coming in there somewhere, right?) Let yourself go a little in the way that music often inspires.

Change your physical writing space, posture, or method. If you write at a desk, sit on the floor. If you write laying in your bed, head outside and find a tree to lean on. If you usually type, try writing by hand. If you usually write by hand, try switching out your pen or pencil for something faster or slower than usual. Give your body a new way to be in this practice and see if it shifts you from overthinking.

Go personal before you go to your work-in-progress. Maybe you have a decade-long to-do list, or maybe you are working through a relationship injury. Maybe you're worried about your child's upcoming concert or maybe you're excited about a friend's impending visit. Those things are beautiful and real, so write into them. Go deep into your emotions about them. Let them guide you to that deep place, and then gently shift your weight into your work without coming up for air. Trust me, there's plenty of room to breathe in your heart.

Here's what I've found from years of practicing this way of writing: it gets easier and richer the more you do it. You probably won't ever master it—at least, I haven't—but the more I go deep, the more I find there's so much more to explore within me.

Why Do We Tell Stories?

I've been carrying this question for days, ever since a friend asked me . . . and I think my answer here is simple. We tell stories because they connect us to one another in a way that even facts and culture and experience sometimes fail to do. They tie us together—barbed and gorgeous, as we are—at the heart.

Much love,
Andi

CHAPTER 33

What's a Writer to Do when Life Is Crushing?

Dear Beautiful People,

This morning, I drove to town to drop something off at our fertility doctor's office because they needed it ASAP. The forty-five-minute drive took over an hour each way, and I came back with my full workday still ahead of me.

As I began work, I noticed water on the floor. After I had ruled out the basset hound, I saw that our roof was leaking . . . steadily with two more days of rain forecast. I grabbed a towel and a bread-making bowl and saved the hardwood floors.

For the past three days, I have been practically immobile with a back injury/misalignment/thing that is so bad that I go into debilitating spasms every time I sit or stand. Philip has had to rescue me several times a day.

Add to that the aftereffects of hormone shots (which I will not go into but make things anatomically uncomfortable) and the ongoing wait to see if we are pregnant, and these are hard days.

But I'm Not Just Writing to Whine

. . . although writing that out does make me feel more justified in my tendency to tears just now. No, I'm sharing all of that with you guys because life is a bit crushing for me just at the moment, and I know it is for some of you, too. Job loss. Chronic illness. Relationship travails. Money shortages. Grief. Mental Illness. Prejudice. Abuse. Life can be very, very hard.

It's at these moments that I think we need to hunker back into our caves and stay out of the rockslide. Sometimes, it's enough to just keep an airhole open and keep going.

For me, I get air by writing. For you, I expect writing may also be life-giving, but so may be sewing or baking or boxing or reading or spending time on the floor with your kids.

This week, if it feels like life is crushing you a bit, step back into the cave of your safe place. (I imagine mine is IN the mountain from which all this debris slid. I can choose to step out into it, or I can do what I need to do to survive and let others manage the debris for a while.) Write what you want with the loosest of goals. Read books you just love. Spend time with people who give you only joy.

Take care of yourselves. Your words need you healthy and well.

Much love,
Andi

CHAPTER 34

The Call to Write

Dear Beautiful People,

When I was young, my parents took my brother and me on a lot of road trips. I would sit in the backseat and stare at the power lines that ran beside the road. My goal was to trace them as far as I could before losing their path.

While I did this, I made up song-stories, lyrics and melodies that rose up as threads from my largely unscarred but tender heart. I sang-spoke my fear, my loneliness (as a bookish, sensitive child, I was pretty lonely), and sometimes my joy. These story-songs gave me a way to work through my emotions and thoughts . . . they were the beginning of my life as a writer.

I Have No Process

I wish I had a step-by-step process to tell you how to kindle your passion for words or music or welding. But I don't. I don't think passions are processed things. They are raw and rugged, cutting and burning from and to the core of who we are.

But here's what got me to a place where I knew I wanted to write for the rest of my life.

I did what I love. I have always loved words. I have been a voracious reader since I was four. I can still remember when a storyteller came to my fourth-grade class, and I sat transfixed as she shared a folktale. I learned about the Trail of Tears from an outdoor drama in Cherokee, NC, and I wept until I couldn't breathe. Words have shaped me in every fundamental way, so it is as natural as breathing for me to turn to them for my living.

I learned to listen to what angers and overjoys me. I get furious when people are told their stories do not matter, when their way of moving in the world is demeaned, when their experiences are not treasured as much as a fact. Then, because I am naturally bent toward words, I found a way to use words to capture those stories, to write into the center of my pain over them (I don't presume to write other people's pain), and to share what I find there. This is why I write about the history and legacy of slavery.

I challenge everything society says I "should" do. I don't eschew personal responsibility or the ways that our relationships give us obligations and duties, but I do challenge—constantly—the idea that I should do this or that. I challenge the idea when it comes to gender, to age, to socio-economic class. Thus, I have felt free to take big risks financially, to take a ninety-degree turn after four years of graduate school, to buy a farm and move to the country where all that education was hard to use in the way society expects I will use it. I choose, instead, to be true to myself, true to other people, and true to what I love . . . and I trust for all the rest.

Maybe You Could Try

I have no words of wisdom about how you find your calling, your passion, your dream beyond what I have said above, but maybe there are some questions you could carry as you consider.

What do you love every time?

What makes you angry or overjoyed?

What obligations do you have to people and society? What obligations can you put aside?

How much of a risk are you willing to take? Financially? Personally?

What could you not live without?

Many of you are writers, and I love being a part of this vibrant community of folks. Some of you are thinking you might like to try this writing thing. Others of us are inching our way toward the writing life. There's no one path here, my friends. There's what you need and want to do that gives your life fullness and meaning, and that—well that looks different for each of us.

So what will you lean into this week with your words? What part of your heart's deepest desire will you allow to speak? What injustice, silence, fragment of laughter will you tie your words around and pull into the light?

Whatever it is that you have to say and in whatever way that happens in your life, I hope you know that I am here cheering you on with my own little fire.

Much love,
Andi

The Call to Bravery

Dear Beautiful People,

During my junior year of college, I studied abroad in England. I had dreamed of that semester for all my teenage years, and the opportunity to do that was one of the reasons I chose that college. I loved everything about that time, including a man I met.

I fell hard for this man, but he didn't choose me. Until he did. Kind of. (It's a long story.) And then until he didn't. When we got back to the US, he broke up with me, and I was absolutely devastated. I cried all the time, and because I had to work alongside this man all summer at our college, I never got distance or perspective.

Long into the fall I ached, mostly silently. I figured I was alone in this, and I would just have to bear it. But one day, the man (who had gone to another campus for the semester) sent me a letter saying I couldn't contact him at all. I got the email in our computer lab (back in the days of DOS-based email), and I broke down. Completely.

At that moment, a blonde-haired man whose name I never learned—even at our tiny college—put his arms around me and held me while I shook with sobs. It was the kindest gesture of love I've ever had from a stranger.

I walked home that afternoon, and my roommate, Molly, was there. As I climbed into my top bunk to cry some more, she climbed up next to me and said, "Andi, you deserve someone who adores you." Then, she sat and let me cry. (Those words would carry me for almost twenty years when I finally met Philip.)

I'm sharing this story for one reason: I want you all to remember that sometimes people can only help us when we ask for that help—whether in words or in tears. If we try to keep ourselves all tightly wrapped together, there's no space for someone to step in and   assist   us.

The Bravery Required to Ask

As writers, we are people kin to solitude. We build ourselves into it and wrap it around us because we need it. Our work thrives in that quiet vapor of aloneness.

But sometimes, sometimes, we wrap ourselves too tight, convinced we can find our way alone. Convinced we MUST find our way alone because that is the way. Or because other people don't care. Or because it looks like everyone else has it all worked out when we are barely holding ourselves together. (You see, of course, that this is not just about writing, except in the way writing is about all of these things, too.)

We do not have to do this work alone, my friends. That's what our community is about. That's what the writers' community is about writ large. We are not isolated in this work . . . unless we choose to be.

But here is what those tears in the computer lab taught me, and here's what sharing about our infertility struggles is showing me: when we ask, people step forward and wrap arms of wisdom around us and help us along.

So this week, I am encouraging us all to ask for one thing that we need for our writing lives.

- Maybe we need to ask our partners or friends to help us keep to the writing times we've chosen.
- Maybe we need to ask for beta readers to give us some feedback on our work.
- Maybe we need to ask friends to sign up for our mailing list.
- Maybe we need to ask a trusted friend or guide for support in the inevitable discouragement that is part of the writing life.
- Maybe we need to ask for help finding an editor or figuring out how to self-publish.
- Maybe we need to ask people to buy our books.

Ask in our writing community. Ask in other writers' groups. Ask in your house. Ask via email. Ask me for something, and I will do all I can to help. Ask someone to help you do one thing.

Be brave, my friends. This is risk, of course, but then, writing that is not risky is not much writing at all.

Much love,
Andi

CHAPTER 36

Today Alone

Dear Beautiful People,

For a few months when I was in high school, I sent someone a letter every single night. From 7:00 to 8:00 p.m.—after dinner and before our family sat down to watch TV—I sat on my bed with one of those really uncomfortable lap desk things with the Formica top and the pillow bottom and wrote a letter. Some of the letters were to people from my high school and some to the guys who attended the local military school in town. Almost none of them were to my good friends . . . maybe because I saw them (although I have no memory of that) and maybe because I felt solid in my few, good friendships but wanted more.

I wrote on college-ruled notebook paper (that wide-ruled stuff is ridiculous!), and I told them about my day, I guess, and asked about theirs, I imagine. I was in the tradition of correspondence that I didn't even know existed but that would become so much of my life . . . history is often told in letters, you see.

Sometimes, my friends wrote me back. Sometimes they didn't. But I wrote, every day, a simple letter. To assuage my loneliness. To connect me to people. To make use of the words that have always swum in my head. (Although in one response, my friend Clyde did suggest that I use the word *awesome* less frequently.)

This was my first lesson in writing discipline, and I taught it to myself.

Living the Daily of Writing

So here's what I'm thinking about for all of us this week: I'm weighing the heft of a day. I'm wondering what we would all find if we took each day—the morning after or the evening of, perhaps—and sketched it in language.

I imagine we'd find wealth and secrets and joy and heartbreaks we knew but didn't see.

For the past five months (I counted as I fed the chickens this morning), I have been working in two-week moments: the days when I'm getting ready to be pregnant and the days I'm waiting to see if I am pregnant. If I've been brave, I've been thinking in nine months and eighteen years, too . . . very little have I been in today, much less now. I'm weary.

So on this day, when I return to my office with a view of our chickens and the companionship of Jelly Roll the cat, on this day when we will drive over the Blue Ridge to get three tiny rabbits, I am leaning back so as not to be leaning forward. I am squaring my hips and settling myself in like a mountain. (I'm standing at my desk in literal mountain pose for those of you who do yoga.)

Might I encourage us all to do the same? Maybe you could write a daily letter to someone, to yourself even. Maybe you just need to fill some journal pages. Maybe daily isn't where you are right now but you could find some time each day to sit and listen to yourself.

So much of the twenty-first century writer's life is about the future, the next book, the big book deal, the big promotion you'll do next month. And so much of what it is to be human is to lean into the past—the book launch that didn't go as we wished, the way that writer or this one didn't support us, the way we wished we started writing so many years ago.

But really, my tender, gentle, word friends, all we have is today, and it is rich enough and strong enough and worry enough for us all.

So this week, maybe you could settle yourselves here in this day, and find what words you have for their own sake. Celebrate them for the fullness and magic that they are. For they are gift received and given, every day.

Much love,
Andi

P.S. If you'd like a practical prompt out of this, try writing about what you experience today to one of these people:

- your mother - dead, alive, unknown to you
- the best friend you have always wanted, whether you have him or not
- a famous figure: the Dalai Lama, the Pope, Lady Gaga, the president of Nigeria

Write a letter each day this week to someone different and stay focused on today—what you see, what you feel, what you consider.

CHAPTER 37

That Time I Stuck My Finger in a Horse's Nose

Dear Beautiful People,

I was about three, maybe two even. I'm sure I had on polyester pants, probably in some shade of green that never appears in nature because, of course, it was 1976 and this is what people wore. My hair was much blonder and finer, and it hung in a bob at my chin. (These were the days before my mother cut it off for being unmanageable and because, she says, I said I hated it.)

Dad had taken me somewhere, just he and I. My brother hadn't yet been born, and I expect Mom needed some time alone. (She would need that for the next twelve years, since I wouldn't leave her side for more than a few hours until hormones pushed me out.) So just Daddy and me. I don't know where we were, but I remember a board fence, three brown boards horizontal between posts. Dad stood me on the second to the top board, and I leaned over into the pasture.

A horse came up—chocolate brown and HUGE to my three-year-old eyes. He nestled up to me, his eyes liquid and soft, and I laughed and promptly stuck my pudgy fist up his nostril.

Then, he bit me.

I screamed, even though I don't remember any blood, and my dad pulled me close as he shook with laughter.

I can distinctly remember thinking that the hole was huge and so it needed my hand in it. I didn't realize it was a nostril, this being the first horse I'd ever seen. I didn't understand why it bit me. I was very mad at that horse.

Now, for how this relates to writing . . . we need to build nostrils in our work. Okay, maybe not nostrils, but caves, tunnels, places where our readers want to poke in their hands or their heads. Concrete, real spaces, emotions, characters, and stories that crave for us to touch them.

The way we create those touchable spots is through scene in prose and imagery in poetry. Scenes and imagery incorporate a few key elements:

Concrete, physical detail.

So we don't say anger. Instead we show her slamming the pedal of the car to the floor as she leaves the parking lot. We don't say that this flower was pretty; we show the way the sun turns it into a thousand shimmers of yellow and the soft points of the petals look sharp enough to cut when we put them against our eyelashes. Concrete detail gives the reader something to taste, touch, hear, see, or smell. A hint--if you find yourself using abstract concepts like love or hope or fear or dread, look for a way to make those concrete.

Setting.

Setting is not just the place that something happens. It is also the timeline., in history and in the day, the weather, the culture, etc. So in a poem, it matters a great deal if the setting is twenty-first century Iowa or fourteenth century Italy or fourth century Nigeria. Setting is crucial, and yet, we often forget to establish it in our work. You can establish setting with subtle things—like cultural materials, music, clothing, or architecture—or you can be more direct and give a year and place as a heading or in the text itself.

Time.

Whether we are writing a memoir or a novel, a poem or an essay, the passing of time in a work is crucial. Time is one of the fundamental ways we locate ourselves as people in the world, so in our writing, we need to help our readers understand the passing of time. Are things happening over the course of weeks or months, or is this one of those moments when only a few seconds actually pass but it feels like the man has been staring at that edge of the picnic table for ten years? You can easily signal time with little phrases: a few days later, on Tuesday, as the bird flew over. Give the reader a way to grab hold of time, and she will manage the work of it for you.

So here's a little exercise. (Don't worry. I'm not going to suggest you go and stick your finger up an animal's nose.) Pick up a book you love and highlight—with a pen or actual highlighter—the elements of concrete detail and scene that you find there. (Yep, really. Mark up the book. You'll see so much more there, and the writer won't mind, I assure you.) Notice the ratio of concrete to abstract. How much telling is happening in the novel versus how much showing? In that poem, what specific, physical things are used and how do they balance against the abstraction.?

Then, look at something you have written recently and see how you have used (or not used) scene and concrete detail. Print it out if needed and highlight things. Mark what is strong and what isn't. Use that piece as a guide to help you improve your future works.

A little highlighter. A little intentional reading. It'll take you far.

Much love,
Andi

P.S. Two years or so after this incident, I was thrown off a pony when I was forced to leave my mom and go to Girl Scout camp, where I cried for seven days solid. Needless to say, there is a reason we don't have horses here on the farm.

CHAPTER 38

Write for the Wonder of it All

Dear Beautiful People,

For thirty years now, whenever I think of peace and rest, I remember an afternoon when I was about twelve. I was at the home of my former piano teacher, Mrs. Fowler, a good friend of my mother. Mrs. Fowler lived across a mountain hollow lane from my best friend, Mary, and for some reason, Mary and I had wandered over from her house to Mrs. Fowler's farm.

I don't know what we were doing that day—some chore or just spending an afternoon. Somehow, we ended up at the edge of the Fowler's yard. It was a warm day—maybe summer in that mountain air—but I wasn't overwhelmed with heat. I was wearing a white shirt with a collar and some sort of red and yellow stitching, very '80s. My hair was cut short, probably asymmetrically as I wore it then. (It's still my favorite hair style for my hair.)

At the edge of that yard, I lay down in the grass, and I folded back my shirt to tan my stomach because, of course, a tan stomach was very important to a girl who had never worn (and still to this day has never worn) a bikini. Then, I stared at the sky and the clouds going by. I watched them pass over the edge of the mountains to my right, and watched them skirt across the valley to the mountains beyond my vision above my left shoulder.

I lay there for hours, long enough to get a really nice four-inch-wide tan-burn line across my stomach. I have no idea what I thought about. No idea if I figured through things or just let my mind travel with the clouds. But when I think of wonder, when I think of rest, when I think of the work of a writer, I think of this afternoon.

The Gift of Wondering

I am one of those people who never grew out of the "why?" stage of childhood, and as annoying as that surely was to my mother and may now be for my friends, I don't chagrin that tendency for a second because it is this propensity to why that makes me a writer.

It is not always easy to carry "why?" around. Sometimes, it would just be simpler to let things be what they are, but that is not how I am built . . . and so I plunge deep into why all the time.

And when I do, I almost always come out into the open skies of wonder, where I find motivations and systems, processes and beauties that I never would have witnessed or let fall against my skin if I had stayed before I asked the why.

So this week, my friends, I encourage you to ask why about something or someone you encounter and then let yourself sink deep into the wondering. Here are some things you might ponder:

- Why do you get so mad when someone does that one thing when you're driving?
- Why do you love that color so very much?
- Why do you remember that afternoon when you were twelve or seventeen or thirty-three?
- Why did you love that first person for whom you felt romantic love?

- Why are you frustrated when people share those kinds of things on Facebook?
- Why do you hate Facebook? Why do you love it?
- Why is that animal one you fear? Or one you love?

Go deep with your why and remember, that in the end, the why is always about you, which is, of course, true for all our writing, too.

Much love,
Andi

P.S. If you'd like to settle into wonder just a bit, watch this video about gorillas and the people who raised them. It broke me open with wonder this morning. -http://en.newsner.com/she-grows-up-with-gorillas-12-years-later-when-theyre-reunited-this-left-me-speechless/about/animals,family.

CHAPTER 39

Moving Between Serendipity and Discipline

Dear Beautiful People,

When I was little, I read this beautiful book along with its companions like *Leo the Lop* (which I clearly need a copy of again) and *Trapper,* after whom my brother named a stuffed seal and I named my current car. These little books with their gentle lessons were fundamental to my childhood. But this one, *Serendipity*, has always been my favorite, probably because it is the name of the book series and is, thus, more weighted and because, well, the word *serendipity* is just wonderful and onomatopoeic. (Another great word.)

But just now, when I pulled up the cover, which is slightly different than the one I had as a child, I read the moral of the story that is at the bottom: "Knowing who you really are will bring you happiness." That alone feels like serendipity. Because, after all, if a writer does not know herself, how does she know what she has to say?

That, however, is another consideration for another letter. Today, I want to talk about the way we live and write in the foggy space between discipline and serendipity.

Serendipity and Discipline

Sometimes I lean way too far into the world of discipline, trusting the regimen, the routine, the practice to do all the work. When I move too far into what feels like the certainty of routine, I can get rigid, unyielding, and blinded to my life, to the vagaries of the story, to opportunity and surprise.

And when I wander too far into the whimsical land of purple dinosaur-water dragon-things named Serendipity, I can lose the path entirely and just sit down and hope someone pushes me to my feet—and to my words again.

For me, the key is to know there is a path on which I need to stay—a schedule, a goal—but to also allow that this path might take me into places, memories, experiences, characters, plot points, word play, or insights that I didn't expect at all.

In terms of practice, this means I need to curtail my natural tendency to be a full-on pantser when it comes to my writing and embrace a bit of my planner self. For you, you may need let the plan slip a bit in favor of what going by the "seat of your pants" might bring.

One Key to All of This

It is hard to write at all if we are too busy, or as Kelly said to me this weekend, if our lives are too full. If every minute of every hour is filled with something we can do or must do or should do or need to do—whew, we have a lot of ways we burden ourselves with doing, huh? —then it is very hard to see the path, much less the whimsy that might lay along it.

So here are a few ways you might try to build in more "white space" on the page of your life and celebrate the silence where idea, inspiration, intersection, and insight lie.

- **In the car, bus, train: walk, don't turn anything on.** Instead of popping in that audio book or your favorite driving mix, sit with the silence. Watch what goes by. Watch what you pass. Pay attention to what captures your attention.

- **Leave open space in your day.** Instead of knowing what you are going to do for every minute of every day, carve out fifteen minutes here or there to just see what comes up. Maybe you'll find you want to stay in a conversation a bit longer. Maybe you'll want to wander around a park. Maybe you'll just want to sit and stare at nothing.

- **Create a mantra that reminds you that doing nothing isn't laziness.** Maybe you need to remind yourself that rest is necessary. Or that color shows up best against a blank background. Or that we miss things when we only look straight ahead. Write down a phrase that reminds you to hold space for surprise and then repeat that phrase to yourself a few times a day.

So I guess, in the end, what I'm offering here is a reminder that we need to walk the between of "some discipline and some serendipity." Our writing gets done when we give it space to happen and to morph into something winged and beautiful, a dragon of words.

Much love,
Andi

P.S. And if you love Mary Oliver as much as I do, maybe carry this with you, too. "You can have the other words—chance, luck, coincidence, serendipity. I'll take grace. I don't know what it is exactly, but I'll take it."

CHAPTER 40

The Rhythms, Oh the Blessed Rhythms

Dear Beautiful People,

I was just standing at my stove stirring tapioca because after a forty-eight-hour migraine, a woman needs pudding—and reading an issue of *Poets and Writers* that has been too long neglected. The first full article was about poet Tess Taylor, and was about how a year working on a farm brought her back to the rhythms of her own work.

She talked about the unpredictability of our springs, and I felt myself tingle because, wow, that hardness, that unsureness about when to put in things that I had been feeling wasn't just in me. She talked about sleeping well after moving rocks all day, and I nodded my head as my right hand stirred. Then, she said, I found myself making up a song as I planted leeks all day long, and I suddenly felt the sway and swoop of the words that come to me when I weed for several hours a day.

Then, I was crying and thinking of you all as I remembered, for the first time in far too long, why I came to this farming life. No, more than that, as I remembered the way I knew—in some part of me that is tied to all human history—that farming would mean writing for me.

The Thing You Do Because You Must

I have been antsy all week because I knew our potatoes and onion sets needed to go into the ground. The adage is that St. Patrick's Day is the day, but with warmer springs, we could actually have done it sooner. Now, it was March 25th, and I had nary a spud in the soil.

So despite a blinding headache, Philip grabbed the furrowing wheel and I the bags of sets. We gathered the scuffle hoe and the traditional one, and we pulled nettle and henbit from the bed before we laid out rows and got these babies into the ground, their sides still wet from Philip's very sharp knife.

While I worked, I felt it—the gentling of my spirit, the way the hard work of preparing soil for food brings something primal and fundamental to life in me. I sat down in the soil and looked for any hint of asparagus and decided to trust instead of to panic when I saw no spear tips.

For me, gardening, tending our animals—oh, the joy of warm eggs and goat nuzzles—of living a life that means I need to be here every night and outside not long after waking. That is the thing I must do to prepare to do the thing I am made to do: write.

For you, it may be making music or spinning wool or spending an hour with your head in the engine of a car. It may be walking a circuit or bending yourself into a triangle. It may be sitting on your front porch and watching the street stories or spending an hour with your grandmother while she talks about the time her mother put her hand through the pocket of a new coat so her father couldn't force its return. Meditation. Acting. The quiet quilting of paint to canvas. Rowing.

Your thing—whatever thing that is that makes it possible for you to do this writing thing. Don't neglect it. Ever.

Watch for its season to come back to you. Watch for it to froth up like foam on strawberry jam. Keep space for it. Turn off the TV. Log off Facebook. Sit on the back deck and sip tea.

Because, friends, when that thing comes to you with the song it makes in your body, then, beautiful people, your words will follow soon—full and loud.

Much love,
Andi

CHAPTER 41

How to Build a Writing Platform with Authenticity

Dear Beautiful People,

If you look up the words "writer" and "platform," you will find as many tips and tricks as there are "experts" in the field. Some folks will tell you to do everything all the time, and some will tell you that you don't really need to build a readership beyond writing good books. The truth, as I've come to know it, is somewhere in between.

And YOUR between is determined by who and how you are in the world. Your platform needs to be only two things: manageable and authentic.

Why Manageability Matters

If you're like me, you have signed up for every new social media option, tried out most marketing tools, listened to podcasts about building an audience until your ears bleed, and felt absolutely overwhelmed by this process and prospect all the time.

Here's what I've learned from experience: I need to learn and try, but I also need to dismiss, discard, and abandon. If I don't, this work of building a platform will shut me down completely, and a shut down writer doesn't write, much less find readers.

Additionally, what you choose to do for marketing and platform-building needs to be consistent, and people that are overwhelmed don't have consistent posting schedules. If you are trying to post five times a day to Twitter, write a blog post three times a week, update your Facebook page twice a day, post a photo to Instagram every day, whisper something into the void that is Ello, keep up with wittiness on Tumblr, AND WRITE as well as maybe work a day job, you're going to fail at doing that consistently. **It's far more important to be consistent with a loose schedule on a few places than to be sporadically present in a lot of places.**

Why Authenticity Matters

Once we've gotten where and what we are going to share managed, it becomes important to think about what we want to share and with whom. We don't have to share a lot of private information about our lives if we don't want to, but we also don't have to only talk about our books or our writing if we'd prefer to be more personal. **The only thing that is required is that we share authentically—from our true selves—and don't fall into the game of trying to be edgy or coy or manipulative with our posts.** (Believe me, that's harder to avoid that you might think.)

So if you really care about politics, want to talk about politics, and feel good having public conversations about politics, then do that. If you would rather not, then don't. If you are comfortable sharing stories from your home life, then do it. If you're not, then don't. You can be as open or as closed as fits you . . . that's what authenticity is about and readers can pick out a sincere person from ten miles out. So don't fake it.

Here's the one caveat: to be successful as a writer you need to be out in the public somewhere. You need to be on social media. You need a mailing list. You need to be engaged with other writers and with readers. So if the authentic you is reclusive and/or shy, that's okay. But you'll need to cultivate a part of your personality that reaches out, even when you'd rather not. Find a few things you can share with readers, and use those as your go-tos. But do share.

My Practices of Platform-Building that I Find Manageable and Authentic

If these suit you, use them. If they don't, ignore them. Or maybe consider your version of these things.

- **I create accounts on most social media sites just so that I have a presence there, but I only post consistently to Facebook, Twitter, and Instagram.** You'll find me on Snapchat and Tumblr, and I even have an Ello page, but I don't do much in those spaces because I simply can't do it all. Instead, I focus my time and energy on the social media spaces that feel most natural to me.

- **I have particular blogging days and newsletter days, and I prioritize those so that I'm sure I'm consistent.** My blogging schedule means that I blog three days a week—one day for each blog (on each different subject). I always blog for Our Folks' Tales on Tuesdays, for Andilit on Wednesdays, and for God's Whisper Farm on Thursdays. Then, I do a newsletter (like this one) for Andilit on the 15th and 30/31st of each month. This schedule means that I can plan ahead and write ahead if I wish, and it allows me to schedule guest posts as well. But more importantly, it places my writing before my readers on a regular schedule that they can know and count on.

- **I work very hard to respond to every comment or email I receive.** I know what it is to feel unheard. I know how it feels to write to someone and never get a reply. I know how much it stings to reach out and get only silence in return. So I do my best to always answer when people write to me, even if it's just posting a <3 on the comment reply.

- **I know which topics I'm willing to share publicly and which I'm not.** If you follow me on FB, you know that my husband and I are working with an egg donor to have a child. We discussed the decision to make that journey public, and I felt it important that I have that support (since I work alone and don't often see people face to face) and wanted to share our story and try to take some of the stigma about infertility away. Some people find that to be too vulnerable for them, and that's just fine. But it works for us. What I don't share on social media is family trials. I don't talk about my relationships with my family members—that's a no-go zone for me.

- **I have pretty strict rules for how I manage my social media pages.** For example, if the first time you comment on something I post is because you disagree with me, I simply delete the comment because I find that rude and disrespectful. You have to earn the right to challenge me, and if I don't know you, you haven't earned that right. I also don't allow name-calling or general ugliness on my page. I reserve the right to delete anything I want without comment. I also set out pretty clear boundaries when I post personal things— i.e., for our fertility posts, I have said I don't want any advice. For the most part, people are respectful of these rules. If they are not, I delete and move on. These rules help me stay engaged and help me protect myself and my friends from ugliness.

If you're new to the world of platform-building, even this letter might feel overwhelming. I completely understand. But remember, if you do you and if you present a true version of yourself with a genuine commitment to respect yourself and your readers, then you'll be fine. Just one step at a time, my friends. One step at a time.

Much love,
Andi

CHAPTER 42

Working the Percentages

Dear Beautiful People,

On Friday, I was talking with a client, and she was sharing how much she felt overwhelmed by all she had to do with her day job, with a new writing opportunity that had come her way, and with her family. It just all felt like too much.

I know that feeling. You probably do, too.

So we talked through some ways to manage overwhelm—pare out what isn't necessary, set boundaries, make a schedule, say no—and then, off the cuff, I told her how I've learned to manage my projects, both for clients and for myself. She found the idea really empowering so I thought I'd share it here.

My Simple Method for Project Management

I suspect many of you do this already, and if I was versed in the literature about project management in general, I'd probably find this advice everywhere. So this isn't exclusive to me or anything.

1. **I find a deadline.** Sometimes my client has a deadline, and sometimes I set it myself, both for my projects and theirs. A deadline is the single-most important tool I use for getting things done.
2. **I count the number of workdays I have to complete the project.** So let's say I want to have a draft of my next book done by June 1st. So that means I have forty workdays to complete the project.
3. **Finally, I break the project down by percentages for each work day.** Thus, if I want to finish a draft of a 50,000-word book by June 1st, I need to write 1,250 words a day. For me, that's manageable, but for you, you may be able to do more or less. If so, adjust the deadline appropriately and do the math again.

How This Method Helps Me
1. **It keeps me from being overwhelmed by the scale of the project.** 1,250 words is far less intimidating than 50,000.
2. **It gives me daily goals for which to aim.** These day-by-day goals keep me accountable and help me move forward. If I'm quicker than I expect, I can work ahead. If I'm slower than I thought, then I know I need to either make up some time or adjust my deadline.
3. **It provides me a sense of accomplishment on a regular basis.** Instead of waiting until the big thing is done to feel like I've actually done anything, these smaller goals help me feel like I'm moving forward, even on the days when I don't do that much.
4. **It keeps me on task.** It's really easy to let a deadline sneak up on me, but this method means that I always have the deadline loosely in mind. Plus, it means that when something unexpected comes up and takes my day, I don't

end up losing the only period of time I set aside for this work.

So there you have it: my method for hitting deadlines, producing work on a schedule, and managing multiple projects.

Much love,
Andi

CHAPTER 43

"The Written Word Is Weak"

Dear Beautiful People,

I was all set to write you an email full of weight about the fullness of our days . . . about too much . . . about overwhelm. But then, I had to open the greenhouse on this warm spring day and to get to the greenhouse I had to walk past our garden. In the garden, I saw pea shoots arriving, and the tiny sprouts of some leafy thing (kale, mustard greens? I don't label well) arriving with the sun's warmth.

Then, I took the chickens some extra food, and by the time I got back to my office, I was calmer and more aware of this thing: **I need to be writing for me just now.**

I need to put aside the idea of a book this summer, or at least take that off the table as my fundamental goal, and instead, just write 1,000 words a day on life as it is in this moment.

Life is full for us now. The farm. The potential for a baby this year. Family moving closer. And words—my own and those of others—spilling out like the water lapping over the edge of the goats' water trough when I walk away for a few minutes.

Writing to the Quiet

For over a year now, I have been writing out loud. Three books last year, hopes for another one this year, editing clients booked months in advance, a writer's retreat that is rapidly filling with amazing folks. It feels like everything I have been writing of late has been about other people, or more specifically, about other people seeing me, seeing my words. All of that writing has been good, and I LOVE all the people I know through this work.

But it's time I write for me for a while. I've been sensing this coming, this quieting off, this pulling inward. But I had been resisting because of what I have taken as truth: that to be successful, I need to be out there, wherever *there* is.

Today's ten minutes in the garden, though, reminded me of something: **I write for myself first and always. That I speak my words because, first, I need to hear them.**

So my *Love Letters to Writers* book, well, I'm going to be setting that aside just for now. It feels like that may be summer work . . . maybe. But here in this spring where so much comes into the light, I need to spend some time seeing it for myself before I shape it up to share with the world.

Inward or Outward: What Do You Need?

I truly believe that if we want to publish, especially if we want to make a full or part of a living as writers, we have to have a public face that is regularly out there in the world. However, sometimes, the public, out loud part of us is small, like a pinky finger waving. Sometimes, though, it's a full-on, wide-armed "Hello, World" posture. (For some reason Liza Minelli comes to mind.) My sense is that none of us can be out loud all the time, though. So today, may I gently ask you a question or two?

Which do you need just now, to be more outward or more inward? And what do you need to change about your life, writing practice, and publication plans to work with that need?

Much love,
Andi

CHAPTER 44

The Power of Momentum

Dear Beautiful People,

We have this basset hound named Mosey. We call him Mo quite often but not because he has much momentum. The final trip outside for the night is more a lesson in inertia.

But watching Mo get riled up—bouncing off the couch, moving every area rug in the house, successfully dislodging safely stored breakables—while he chases our other hound Meander is a reminder to me that **once someone gets going, they are hard to slow down.**

Mo-mentum for Writers

If you've read much of what I've written about the writing life, you know that I hate rules that are applied across the board for all writers. I just don't believe they work. But I do believe there are a few principles or guidelines that are typically true for most of us.

One of those is the principle of momentum. In terms that would make Newton and all other physicists squirm, the idea of momentum is that once you get going you keep going. (Think of that in a James Brown- type rasp, and you'll grasp the full feeling.)

For writers, momentum means that we are more likely to keep writing if we get some rhythm going, if we do it regularly, if we engage with words on some sort of schedule. There's something about getting a pattern of sitting at the page that makes us want to come back again and again.

Of course, the opposite is also true: the longer we stay away the easier it is not to come back to words.

Three Things I Do to Keep Momentum

Every writer is different, so take these ideas if they are helpful to you:

- **I write on a schedule.** Sometimes, that means I write every weekday from 10:00 a.m.to12:00 p.m. Sometimes, it means that I write on a certain blog on a certain day of the week or send out my newsletter on certain dates. Or I ask folks for deadlines or set my own to keep me moving forward. A schedule keeps me accountable to getting things done and helps me keep my writing momentum going.

- **I write with goals in mind.** On those days when I'm writing from 10:00 a.m.to12:00 p.m., I write 1,000 words each day without fail. When I do that regularly, I get a rhythm going, and my body and mind just know how long that will take and how much energy. So when I sit down, it feels manageable to do that much.

- **I protect my time.** I know I say this all the time, but it's true: the best thing I do for my writerly momentum is honor my schedule, unless there's a true emergency or I purposely schedule time off. Otherwise, I'm writing to my schedule no matter what—no matter the invitation out to see friends, no matter my lack of energy because Baby Flobo (what we call the baby growing inside me right now) is stealing my life force, no matter the household chores that need doing. I find a schedule that I can keep, and I keep it . . . it's absolutely necessary for me to do so if I want to build writerly momentum.

I don't know what works for you: going someplace in particular to write regularly, putting on a particular soundtrack, having a certain beverage at hand—but whatever keeps your writer Mojo Momentum going, do it. It may be the best thing you do for your writing life.

Much love
Andi

147

CHAPTER 45

Looking for the Silver

Dear Beautiful People,

I once had a man I dated tell me after I broke up with him—that I didn't want to be with him because I didn't want to be happy . . . "You want to be sad so you can have things to write about."

That was one of the cruelest (not to mention self-centered) things anyone has ever said to me, but he was right about one thing: writing is easier for me when I'm cracked open by the pain of life. *

Right now, I have been peeled back to the bone by the loss of the pregnancy Philip and I worked so hard to achieve. I am okay, truly, but I am deeply sorrowful.

This morning, though, as I washed cucumbers and marveled at the first yellow tomatoes from the garden, I realized this—this grief has pulled back from the layers of life that were clouding my view on writing and, more specifically, what I want to write in this world.

So today, I'm finding the silver—not in the lining because the metaphor there is far too direct—but in the underneath swirl that arises when life flips you over so you're staring at your feet against the clouds.

Some of you are in bright, warm days when all feels goodness and joy. Some of you are in dark days where light is a promise you can't bear to even reach for.

So here's my gentle suggestion for you: look for the silver. It may glimmer behind those clouds or you may have to dig hard for it in the muck of disappointment. Look for it, and then stare at it . . . study the contrast of that shimmer against the shadow. Maybe just for a minute. Then, study the shadow because a writer sees it all and writes the truth of it, relief and acceptance, all in one breath.

Much love,
Andi

*Please note that I'm not advocating sorrow as a writing tool. I am simply sharing what I have found to be true for me. If you access your truest self during great joy, that's absolutely amazing, and I'm jealous.

CHAPTER 46

Bald, Baby Heads and Tears

Dear Beautiful People,

Last night, Philip and I went to a gathering at one of my dearest friends' houses. I was excited for her, for this first get-together at her new home, for the chance to see friends, for time out in the summer that didn't involve work. But I was also nervous because I knew another friend—a friend who is six months pregnant with twin boys—would be there. I wasn't sure how I'd react to seeing her, well, more specifically to seeing her pregnant body.

But it was beautiful when she walked in. We locked eyes, and I smiled, and she smiled with a frown and said, "How are you?" And I remembered I loved her and was excited for her, and she remembered I was sad. That's friendship.

What I Didn't Prepare For

I had braced myself about my pregnant friend. I had planned things to say and ask. I had prepared to be gracious. And I didn't even need all that prep because I know my friend and adore her.

But when Philip and I walked back up from the fishing pond and I saw the powder-white head of a baby against his mama's chest, I felt my knees swing outwards. I quietly said, over my shoulder to Philip, "There's a baby up here." I felt like I was warning him. I was mostly warning myself.

When we reached the house, I smiled at the baby's mom and realized, when a toddler joined her, that I knew her husband through our mutual friends. Then, I told Philip that we'd say goodbye and head out. "Okay," he answered.

I held it together for good-byes and a few hellos as people arrived. I hugged my dear, dear friend and thanked her. I got in the car and sighed.

I held it together when we picked up dinner, although we used a drive-through because, well, babies might be inside. I held on until we were home and chores were done, and I was standing in the kitchen while Philip finished mowing the grass.

Then, I sobbed against the counter.

The Way Writing Catches You Unbraced

The talented writer and my precious friend Gayle Brandeis once told me that when you read a piece aloud and find yourself choking up you know, then, you're writing the truth.

That wisdom has carried me far, when I read in public and when I read my own work out loud . . . but what Gayle didn't tell me, probably because she knew I already knew, was that the truth of what you are writing probably won't be what you expect it to be. You'll probably be braced to tell that story of the time of your abuse or of the loss of your brother. You'll probably practice and be fortified for the hard memory of a broken heart or the time your dog fought off a raccoon for you and died as a result. You'll probably be ready for tears when you talk about your child's first words or the way your partner looked at you when you came down the aisle.

But there will still be things in your writing that will take your breath and send the tears to the corners of your eye-windows. It may be the way you describe a flower or the memory of your mom farting every time she laughed too hard (that one always gets me). Or you may feel your throat tighten when you think back on the time someone was rude to you in third grade. Maybe your stomach will clench unexpectedly when you're journaling about your day and realize that the person who cut you off in traffic, well, you weren't really mad at her but at the way you feel you've let people take advantage of you for years.

When we write, we open ourselves, we peel back the protective coverings of rehearsed memories and staid responses. We become vulnerable—in those moments when we do this writing thing with all of ourselves—and we find new joys and new sorrows that we have yet to understand.

Perhaps that is why Flannery O'Connor said, "Anybody who has survived his childhood has enough information about life to last him the rest of his days." Because it's never all explored. It's never all understood. It's never all fresh.

So brace yourselves, friends, for the things you know will hurt when you write them. Care for yourselves so that you don't re-harm yourself in the writing. But also know that one of the great beauties of writing is that it takes you places for which you cannot be prepared, and it helps you find hope there.

After the sobs subsided, I took out my journal, and I wrote so hard that I forgot to think. I poured out the tears and the anger. The pain. I pushed into why that bald baby head left me wrecked. I thought of Elizabeth McCracken's stunning memoir *An Exact Replica of a Figment of My Imagination* and let her story help me tell mine. Someday, I will go back and read those words. I will remember how they helped me now, and I imagine I will find myself broken open to fresh healing again then.

That, my friends, is the worth of writing.

Much love,
Andi

CHAPTER 47

Garlic, Ritual, and My Return

Dear Beautiful People,

I spent a few blessed minutes in our garden this morning. I wrapped my still-sleepy fingers around golden and red tomatoes. I rescued an almost-too-large cucumber from the shadow of her own leaves. I gave the tomatillos a gentle squeeze and harvested those that were ready for salsa verde.

Then, I wandered up to the green beans and began to harvest. The slowness of the motion, the repetitive work of tugging food from vine, always gives me space to really find what I'm feeling. Earlier this week, grief made himself known over the green beans. Today, resentment and a bit of anger sparked up.

I felt myself angry about the way I've let so much of my life become centered around something I could not control (and then I let that go because, well, I'm living some big things right now.) I felt myself angry at people who were asking me for things (usually reasonable things but also sometimes not) in one of the hardest weeks of my life. I felt myself angry, though, mostly at the way life is hard sometimes, at the way if bites you in the leg and drags you down, leaves you there in the dirt, and makes you content with being there.

So it's time to make some changes.

Saying Yes to the Routines and Rituals that Give Me Life

Our farm is often the thing that saves my life. The thought of chickens pecking each other relentlessly propels me out of bed most days at dawn. The fact that our rabbits go almost frantic with joy when I feed them and that I must stand between our goat Bliss and our other girls so they get some feed gets my body moving. The promise of fresh food for ourselves and our neighbors helps me get my body bending . . . that's the first part of my day in the warm weather, and I love it.

The promise of coffee laced with cinnamon (even if it is decaf these days), the clean page of a journal I bought in Palmer, Alaska, the chance to breathe and read, and stare out the window—they all help me settle into my heart when I return to the farmhouse.

A candle lit on my desk. A new page of the Farmer's Almanac calendar read and reminding. The standing desk Philip made me ready to go. One thousand words there through my fingers. That's the most important work I do all day.

The Choice to Live This Way

I have chosen a way of life that gives me ultimate freedom. I choose my schedule most days, and I can take a day off without major consequence. But when I let myself walk away from the life I have chosen, when I give into the weight of life and instead of choosing the unbearable lightness, when farm and animals become burden instead of gift, I have turned away from what I have chosen.

The only way I know back is through tiny rituals of word and deed. It is not always easy to turn back, to return to my center.

Inertia is a mighty force, but mightier still is calling and vocation and the way that 1,000 words written true and clear as I can makes me alive to all that is around and within me.

This afternoon, I will staple up twine beneath the lean-to on our potting shed, and I will listen to birdsong as I hang hundreds of bulbs of fresh-dug garlic. I will let their scent and the whispery song of their wrappings tell me stories and lead me back, one clove and one word at a time.

May you have the rituals and routines that you need to find your way to words as often as possible.

Much love,
Andi

CHAPTER 48

I Knew Every Room

Dear Beautiful People,

I grew up in the church. Literally. My mom was the church music director (Sundays and Wednesday nights), and she also used the piano in the choir room to teach piano lessons after school four days a week. I probably spent as many waking hours in that brick Presbyterian building as I did at home.

I knew every corner of that building: the big, gabled room that was the four and five-year-old's Sunday school classroom, the long L of a hallway that went back to the furnace room where they stored extra tables and chairs, the double doors painted dark brown that led from the storage room to the parking space where Mom always parked in the second space, never the first.

But when I recall this building, the space that most often comes to mind is the balcony above the sanctuary. More specifically, the narrow hallway beside the raked rows of pews. The hallway between the low wall around the pews and the closet with the door cut to fit the angle of the roof.

I have no special memory of that place except that I think that closet may have gone out to the other side by the staircase. There was no trauma in that space and no great game of hide and seek that ended magically or tragically. It's just the space that first comes to mind when I think of that building, the building I always felt safest in.

Hunkering Down in Memory

Later this week, I will be traveling to the part of the world where that church stands so that I can be a part of a panel at the Wild Goose Festival. I'll give my talk, and then, I'll take Philip around the world in which most of my ideals and prejudices took shape. I will take him back to the church. We will at least drive by.

I know the pastor there now. He was a youth group leader when I was a child, and the lesson I most remember him teaching us was how people are wont to do what they are told not to do. He illustrated that story by telling us about the time his mom told him not to put green beans up his nose. I expect Patrick would be mortified to know that I carried that away as his greatest teaching.

But all that said, I could write and ask if the building might be open for me to walk through. I haven't been there in almost thirty years, but the very thought of it brings tears to my eyes.

Here's the thing, though. I don't know if I want to see what IS. I'm scared to lose my memory, scared to see that things are smaller or more worn or not as "all aglow" as they were when I was a kid. I kind of want to hunker down in the rosy shades I created.

Writing into the Truth

But if there's one thing I've learned in this living and wording journey it's this: the truth is worth the risk. It's worth walking through the fear, living with the disillusionment, and seeing things for what they are. So I have just written Patrick to see if Philip and I can visit . . . and I'm still scared but also excited, but I imagine there's something there for me about the balance of memory and the shape of really seeing, something about the way childhood tells one truth and adulthood another. I may just be able to finish the piece I've been carrying around about that church for ten years.

So this week, my friends, my gentle challenge to you is that you go back into a childhood memory, maybe even a treasured one, and look for the truth you couldn't see with your child's eyes then. Turn that memory around. See it as you are now. What do you find there? More beauty? Some pain? A little destruction of an idol? Maybe a little healing?

I don't know what your journey will hold, but I know that going in for the truth with our words is always the best thing, even when it scares us.

Much love,
Andi

CHAPTER 49

Writing Because of Now

Dear Beautiful People,

My grandmother is twenty days shy of ninety-two years old. Until April, she had lived every day of those ninety-one years within three miles of the house in which she was born. Because she needed us to, even if she didn't want us to, we moved her to Virginia to be near her only living family. She is lonely. She was lonely there.

Most days when I visit her, the conversation eventually turns the gentle corner toward what Grandma thinks when she wakes. "Every morning I wake up and ask the Lord to take me. 'Take me home,' I say.'"

She is ready, but she is still here.

Grandma has set her eyes on the endgame, feeling as if here she has nothing left on which to gaze. I am sad for her, tragically sad. She is so sad for herself.

Recently, Sherman Alexie cancelled the rest of his book tour because he found that he needed to grieve his mother, the person about whom his memoir is written.* He found himself followed by his mother's ghost, and he found his grief overwhelming him. So he stopped.

He took the choice to tend the now of who he is instead of the then of his business, of his fans, of his work.

I admire that.

I am a Type 2 on the Enneagram, and one of the fundamental features of a 2 is that we look forward to things, often at the detriment of what is happening, who is with us, and where we are now. When I read of this characteristic of 2s, I sighed . . .*Yes, that's me.*

I am the person who began packing for college a full three months before she left because I was so excited and found herself overwhelmed by the first days of actually being there. I am the person who looks forward to the new movie only to find it unable to live up to my expectations. I am the person, who when waking on a morning after a lovely vacation and feeling the weight of the life in which she lives, begins to think about how she can save for retirement.

But here is what I have learned in the grief-heavy hours of my life: I cannot predict what will come. I cannot count on it. I cannot live for it . . . because it may not be there, and even if it is, it may not be what I expected or needed.

It is so easy to become focused on the "when this" of writing. When I finish this book, when I have 500 subscribers, when I get my first royalty check, when I can make a living freelancing, when my book hits the bestseller's list . . . it's so easy to push our gaze ahead and look forward to those things.

But let me tell you as someone who has accomplished all those particular what-ifs but still has a million more, they are always disappointing if they are the focus. Always.

So I've learned that I must focus on the page, focus on today's 1,000 words, focus on this post or this letter or this article or this poem. Because only here, in the tiny gaps of air beneath our hands and the black and white of our words, here is what we can control. Here is what gives us meaning . . . the practice of our writing, not our products.

When I visited Grandma last week, she and I talked about her favorite book, the Bible, and I reminded her how in Ecclesiastes 11, it says, "Take delight in each light-filled hour." She nodded and looked to the window. "That's what I'm going to do," she said.

Then, she sighed and stared off ahead of her again.

Much love,
Andi

CHAPTER 50

What It Feels Like to
Sign a Book Contract

Dear Beautiful People,

Last week, I printed out and then signed my first-ever traditional book contract. I've been working with two men—one posthumously using his manuscript—to complete a book about racism in the church. I'm co-writing this title, and I'm thrilled to be a part of this important writing. I'm also bolstered by the affirmation in my writing skill that a traditional contract confers.

In fact, I was so over the moon that just the act of signing that piece of paper brought me to tears so intense that I had to stop and just cry for a few minutes.

Yet, this morning, on a day when many of my fellow Americans (I felt very presidential writing that, I'll have you know) are enjoying the Labor Day holiday, I am working just as I have worked every Labor Day since I began living the life of a full-time writer. This is the work.

The writing isn't easier because of this contract. I don't suddenly have more time in the day (in fact, I have less since I'm now on deadline for revisions). I don't now feel perfectly confident in my writing prowess. I don't have a million dollars in the bank. It's still just me and the page.

A bit anticlimactic, I know. And yet, also just right.

I'm very happy, and I'm doing the same thing: writing every day. That's the work, my friends. That's the work.

Much love,
Andi

CHAPTER 51

The Lessons of the Trees

Dear Beautiful People,

My father is named Woody, and he ran a tree nursery for most of my adult life. He has always appreciated trees, especially the monumental ones who have stood for centuries and the unusual ones that have stretched and turned and dug themselves in to survive. From my earliest days, I remember him pointing me toward those trees, "Look at that, Andi. See how it twists to reach the light."

This weekend, as Philip and I drove the flat, tree-lined roads of Eastern Virginia, I watched for the trees. We saw a giant sycamore—probably 300 years old—in Lancaster by a tavern built in the late 1700s. I stretched up straight and strong toward the sky. I wanted to hug it.

We saw cedars laden with berries growing beside the brackish waters of a cover on the Rappahannock and marveled that they could tolerate the salt water as they leaned out over it.

We saw archways of deciduous beauties arcing their arms over roadways so old that they had carved their way like water does in canyons. They shifted themselves toward the light, making a perfect tunnel for our tiny white car.

Because I have grown up loving and appreciating trees, they are often significant reminders for me, reminders to put down good roots where I am, to grow toward the light, to battle for my existence even in adverse conditions because I am the only one of me.

So today, friends, where you are—with all the demands on your time and energy, with the way obligations and fears block much of the light, with the waters of time ebbing over your feet—grow into your words. We can always find reasons not to write: too much to do, too much stress, too much shame, too much fear, too much ambition, too much _____, but we can also choose to find our way in our words even in dark alleys on brackish waters.

Writers for centuries have done so, and while we may not know all of their words, lost as they are in the stories of oppression or silencing, in the sands of writing that are lost to time, but we know those writers—as well as the famous ones—were there, recording, finding their truth in the arc and twist of letters.

So today, friends, root deep. Take your nourishment where it comes. Stretch toward the light. Find a way. Your words are needed.

Much love,
Andi

CHAPTER 52

Writers, It's Okay to Make Money and Be Famous

Dear Beautiful People,

When we first got this farm, I really struggled because I now owned fifteen acres of beautiful Virginia countryside AND a 200+-year-old farmhouse AND goats AND chickens AND dogs AND cats. It felt like abundance, and in my life—largely through some misguided teachings from the faith of which I am a part—I felt like abundance was not something I was supposed to have. I was supposed to be poor because if I wasn't, I was being selfish.

I was operating out of what people in the Christian church often call "the poverty mindset." I wanted to act like money didn't matter, that the lack of money was what was important. I wanted to pretend like the way God operates is by handing us things in little packages that don't require us to work for them and that having money was a sign of my greed.

I know better, but I don't always act better. That's true for my writing life, too, and I know it's true for many other writers, too.

Recently, I have had writers say all of the following to me:

- I don't really care about money.
- I don't really want more readers.
- I think marketing my work is self-centered.
- I don't write my books to sell them.

I cringed at every utterance because, well, I've said all those things myself. But here's the truth: **Money matters.** It doesn't have to be our top priority, it probably shouldn't be our primary focus in anything, and we need to be ethical about how we acquire money. But it does matter.

Let me see if I can give you an example from my very real life. Right now, I am working on a book called *Plantation Jesus* for a publisher. I did get a small advance, glory be, but that advance just came yesterday, when I finished almost all the work on the book. That meant I had to take time away from other work to finish it. That was hard, and it meant a lean early part of September for Philip and me. . . so lean that we have $25 to make it about a week.*

Or consider this book. I need $400 for a cover design, at least $300 for an editor, $125 for an ISBN, plus other miscellaneous funds to pay for graphics, templates, etc. That's at least $1,000 just to get the book into the world. (That's a low budget for a self-published book, by the way.)

These books wouldn't be possible if I didn't make money from what I do. If I didn't charge a fair and reasonable amount to edit, if I didn't sell copies of my books, if I didn't have Patreon supporters, and if my husband didn't have a full-time job with a salary and benefits, none of this would be possible. **I need money to be able to live into my calling as a writer.**

(And don't even get me started on the cost of feeding and caring for all the critters on this place.)

Here's the thing: **I believe that what I do as a writer (and as a farmer) is important.** I believe that the Christian church needs the book on racism that *Plantation Jesus* is. I believe that writers need the encouragement and commiseration I'm going to give in *Love Letters*. I believe that because I feel the pull to write them in the truest part of my heart, and I believe that because people have told me that my *Steele Secrets* books and *The Slaves Have Names* have mattered to them. I also believe people really love fresh turnips.

So, my dear, beloved writers, please stop believing you need to be a starving artist. Please stop acting as if money is evil (it's the "love of money" from Scripture, remember). Please stop giving up your healthy goals and dreams for book sales and income to support yourself.

We don't believe that Toni Morrison or Kevin Kwon shouldn't make a living at what they do. We don't believe that A.S. Byatt should be destitute as she writes her next novel or that Margaret Atwood should live on packets of cheap ramen while she pens her next post-apocalyptic masterpiece. If we don't believe that for writers we admire and love, why in the world would we believe it for ourselves.

I want people to read my words, and I want people to buy them. And with all my heart, I want that for you, too.

Much Love,
Andi

*By the way, in case it needs to be said, I know how very privileged I am economically. I don't take that for granted at all, and I try in every way I can to share what I have. Always.

Epilogue

Beloved writers, thanks for reading through a couple of years of joys and really hard stuff with me. I hope these words have heartened you, have stiffened your resolve, have helped you hold grace for yourself. I hope after reading them you feel more ready to embrace who you are as a writer in the world . . . because as I've said time and again in these pages, we need your words, your stories, the way you see life. We really do.

If **you'd like to join the AMAZING group of writers to whom most of these letters were written, we welcome you. Visit https://andilit.com/online-writing-group/ to sign up.**

Other Books by Andi

Writing Books

Writing Day In and Day Out: Living a Practice of Words

Discover Your Writing Self: 31 Days to Deeper Understanding of Who You Are as a Writer

Other Titles

God's Whisper Manifesto: The Makings of a Dream

The Slaves Have Names

Steele Secrets

Charlotte and the Twelve: A Steele Secrets Story

ABOUT THE AUTHOR

Andi Cumbo-Floyd is a writer, editor, and writing coach who lives at the edge of the Blue Ridge Mountains with her husband, four dogs, four cats, three rabbits, six goats, and thirty-six chickens. She writes regularly at www.andilit.com.

46281026R00104

Made in the USA
Columbia, SC
27 December 2018